Tasty
Lutefisk
Publishing

ANCHORAGE, ALASKA

BLOOD PISS & CHEER

ALASKA

Seldom does a man get to live his dream.

Kristian H. Erickson

Tasty
Lutefisk
Publishing

ANCHORAGE, ALASKA

ISBN: 978-1-7358135-2-3 (Paperback)

ISBN: 978-1-7358135-7-8 (Hardcover)

Tasty Lutefisk Publishing Anchorage, Alaska

Cover photo courtesy of Paxson Woebler, Anchorage, Alaska https://winterbear.com/photography/Creative Commons BY 2.0 https://creativecommons.org/licenses/by/2.0

Original pen and ink and watercolor drawings by the author, photography by Matt Faubion, Anchorage, Alaska

Cover design: Marc Heriot, Marana, Arizona

Interior design: Lizzie Newell, Anchorage, Alaska

Contents

Dear Reader,

French Kissing in an American Cult, published in 2020, told of my descent into a leadership role in a right-wing Pentecostal mega-church. The final chapters reveal that my soul escaped and all was well. I promised you, the reader, that the next book would be different, a compendium of stories of Western Washington mountaineering, emergency medical first-response, and of my dream to be in the land of my pioneer heritage, Alaska. This book is romantic idealism and bloody tragedies, coupled with self-deprecating humor.

I was hired at Seattle's PEMCO Insurance Company in 1988, and that company was my resuscitation into real-world dignity and tolerance after the lunacy of the cult. A few months after I started work there, a

Human Resources representative told me about their troubled deliberations over my job application. I was the best candidate for the job, she said, but the hiring committee was at an impasse because of my résumé. Community Chapel and Bible Training Center, where I had been a leader for 19 years, was still a hot topic in tabloid journalism while month by month bizarre stories appeared in print and on TV. One team member stood to her feet and said in my defense, "Remember that they fired him." I was thankful for that advocate because she was the reason I got the job. After putting so much work into my curriculum vitae, it was humiliating to think that my strongest asset was the fact that I got fired.

I hope that you, too, will find inspiration and redemptive ironies in the following stories.

Kristian H. Erickson
Anchorage, Alaska

Part One
Ayagneq

Yup'ik Eskimo language, meaning
"the beginning"

Wind-tortured Sitka Spruce on Mitkof Island,
above the Wrangell Narrows.

1

Muktuk Buffet

Thursday, December 21, 1995, was my last day of work at PEMCO Insurance Company in Seattle. Over seven years, I had made every effort to do the best work I could, and at the same time amass credentials that would make me attractive to a future employer in Alaska.

In PEMCO's Subrogation/Legal unit, when someone retired or otherwise left the company in good standing, the tradition was to schedule a going-away luncheon at the nearby Space Needle restaurant. But feeling that would be too ostentatious, I requested that we have an in-house potluck, instead. Every subro staffer could bring their favorite dish into the office for all-day snacking. I told the department I would be bringing something special, too.

On the day of the potluck, Building Operations had set up two linen-skirted tables and a series of power outlets next to our cubicles. Crock pots of spaghetti and Swedish meatballs soon appeared, along with lasagna and green salads, complemented by cookies and cakes. On the corner of one table there was a gift for me, a hardbound copy of Toynbee's *A Study of History*. On the frontis piece inside, my Subrogation buddy Robert Korman had written this dedication, "Seldom does a man get to live his dream."

With each visit to Alaska over the previous years, my commitment to making the move north had further solidified. One of my fondest memories was a vacation with my son Evan to see migratory birds near Nome. While there, I asked a dear Inupiaq Eskimo woman, who ran Olson Air Service, if she could help me find a couple pounds of muktuk. She said she had some in her freezer, and that the slab had come from a recent whale harvest in Savoonga on St. Lawrence Island. I went to the Alaska Commercial Company's store and bought an insulated cooler for its trip back to Seattle.

Muktuk (or mangtak in Yup'ik) is the first couple inches of whale skin and blubber, most commonly harvested from bowhead (arveq) whales. The skin looks a lot like a scuba-diver's wetsuit, only thicker. As one might expect, it is chewy, rubbery, and mostly flavorless, though the blubber (whale fat) underneath is sweet. Muktuk is an Alaskan Inupiat food of celebration, so it seemed appropriate for my last day at PEMCO. It is eaten raw, usually cut into squares or strips.

The day before my farewell potluck, I took the muktuk out of the freezer and I pulled out my soon-to-be ex-wife's enormous crystal platter. I woke up early to cut the muktuk into cubes that I then arranged it in a floral pattern on the platter, garnishing all with fresh parsley. I set the arrangement in an ice-filled cake box. That morning, I didn't take my usual Metro bus; instead, I drove and parked in the Visitors Only zone on the top floor of the garage. Security might ticket me, but what were they going to do, fire me?

The muktuk stayed on ice between canapés and celery sticks. Bold colleagues tried it and liked it, while others said that the fish-flavor was too peculiar and strong. Everything was going, er, swimmingly until noon when the last of the ice melted, leaving the crystal platter floating in melted ice water. As the warming muktuk began to smell, word spread throughout the building that there was whale blubber on the third floor. Staffers from other departments stopped by to sample some or simply to gawk. But the light-hearted atmosphere quickly shifted when a group came up from the first-floor sales unit to protest the flesh of an endangered species being consumed.

The odor permeated half of the third floor. A pregnant lady—susceptible to strong smells—became nauseous, and her supervisor gave her the afternoon off. Another woman returned from the ladies' room after trying a piece, saying that she had gone there to vomit. Nobody was getting any more work done.

Everett, a gifted entertainer with a day job in the cafeteria, came up one floor to strut his stuff. He was still clad in his white apron, but he might as well have been wearing sequins and heels. Putting the palms of his hands to his cheeks, he shrieked, "Oh, no, Namu, tell us it isn't you!" referencing the killer whale immortalized in the 1966 film.

Fortunately, once all the muktuk had been eaten, the smell had mostly disappeared. I was packing up the platter and cake box, along with my personal belongings when a director in PEMCO's hyper-organized HR department suddenly appeared. The Company was not pleased with my stunt, she said stiffly. My actions had cut into the productivity of dozens of staff members that day. She told me that if I were coming to work the next morning—she knew that I wasn't—she would have ordered me to appear for a hearing regarding probation. I had trouble suppressing a smile at her remarks. Back at home that evening, I washed the crystal platter and put it back in the cupboard. I never told Melinda what it had been used for that day.

On my first day as a former PEMCO employee, Friday, December 22, 1995, the sun was setting over Bellingham Bay as I drove my candy-apple red Suzuki Sidekick to the Alaska Marine Highway check-in office. They gave me a big sticker for my windshield labeled HAINES, the Alaska port of call where I would disembark the following Monday night. I parked to wait on the pier in front of the stern car-deck doors of the MS Matanuska, scheduled to depart at 8 PM. The ship was being refueled, cleaned, and loaded with foodstuffs for its two galleys, one for crew and another for passengers.

The harbor was a bit more than an hour north of Shoreline, the Seattle suburb where I had lived. That morning, I had directed three movers loading my half of the marriage's household furnishings into a 10-foot-long Conex unit, an ocean-going shipping container. To thank the fellows for their work, I drove to the Washington State Liquor Store adjacent to the grocery store I'd shopped at for years and bought three Christmas-festooned fifths of imported Scotch whiskey. I wished them a Merry Christmas.

Three months earlier, I had taken the trepidatious Alaska insurance licensing exam monitored by a proxy-agency in Bellevue, Washington. Being almost over-prepared, I succeeded on my first attempt, and minutes after the scoring I received a congratulatory email from Alaska Governor Tony Knowles. The license meant I could now accept the most important job offer of my lifetime, working as an adjuster at Wilton Adjustment Service in Anchorage.

The little Suzuki was loaded to the roof with the treasures I didn't feel comfortable committing to a container on a ship crossing the North Pacific in January. Among them was a 19th century hand-etched glass "Krug," a 14-inch-tall wine decanter with a pewter Prussian eagle on top. Under an engraving of a knight on horseback was the inscription, "*Jeden Feind besiegt der Deutsche, doch den Durst besiegt er nicht.*" (The German conquers every enemy, but thirst, never.) I had acquired this treasure on a trip to communist East Berlin in 1973. Unlike most other fragile items in Hitler's capitol city, this object had survived the World War II bombings unscathed, and I was determined to see that its good luck continued.

Toward the bottom of the load in another cardboard carton was a two foot-long cribbage board, a walrus tusk adorned with intricate ivory figures depicting a seal hunt. The piece culminates in the head of a roaring polar bear, and it is to this day one of the finest such pieces of Bering Sea coastal art I have ever seen. Laid flat on top of everything, just below the dome light and wrapped in the blanket I had purchased during my first week at the University of Freiburg in Germany in 1967, was the most cherished item of all—a 3' x 4' privately-commissioned oil painting of Denali as seen from Wonder Lake.

Both the tusk and the painting belonged to my uncle Andrew Longmire, who himself factored into Alaska territorial history. In visits to my uncle's house from childhood into adulthood, I had shown special admiration for the two pieces of Alaskana. Andrew had obviously taken note of my interest, because when his will was read, they were both designated for me. Uncle Andrew also willed his money to his nephews, and for me it was enough for a down payment on a dream home on the southern edge of Anchorage, with views of the vast and mountainous Chugach State Park. For several years, I maintained it as a rental property as my plans to move to Alaska took shape. I never imagined that my wife wouldn't be coming with me.

I believe that the struggle that ultimately ended 19 years of marriage came down to Melinda's need to maintain her own unique identity. Given that she was a talented skier who later became an adept mountain climber and had studied German in college, we had multiple passions in common. I was also attracted to the fact that she had spent her childhood in Alaska. I ended up proposing to her on the summit of Mount Rainier, at the precise place where my great uncle Len Longmire had brought his girlfriend Fay Fuller back in 1890. Fay was the first woman to ever reach the summit of Rainier, and though Melinda's ascent was considerably less dramatic, I suppose my elation was just as grand as his. For the two decades that followed the 1890 climb, Len was Rainier's only climbing guide, charging tourists a dollar each to go from Camp Muir to the 14,410-foot summit. In my thinking at the time, standing atop the summit with Melinda, all the necessary pieces for a long and happy marriage seemed to be there.

However, over the years, this lovely and intelligent woman, the mother of our son, Evan, pushed back against the perceived expectation that she needed to be a carbon-copy of me. We had married in an ultra-fundamentalist church where it was demanded that wives must submit to their husbands in all things. I cannot imagine how difficult it was for her to go against this misogynist philosophy. I recall times when her frustration boiled over, for example, when she exclaimed, "Kristian, you're obsessed with Alaska!" Without being rattled, I replied, "I'm not obsessed. I'm focused." Melinda was not impressed.

The divorce took a year to finalize, as required by Washington State law. In 20/20 hindsight it is hard to imagine that the catalyst for the breakup was not the fact that I had suppressed being a homosexual. I was a devoted husband and good dad. Over the course of my 25 years in fundamentalist Pentecostalism, I had thoroughly polished my acting skills. I deceived most others about who I really was, and I essentially convinced myself that I was straight. Whatever my thought process, I considered my marriage vow to be sacred, and I kept it.

The attorney who crafted the Washington State Parenting Plan determined that it would be best for our son if I became the custodial parent in Alaska, while she would be responsible for summer and holiday visitations in Seattle. Evan had been a skier since age 2, and he'd come to live in Alaska with me, a place he'd visited multiple times and had developed a fondness for. A week before my drive to Bellingham, before turning on her heels and letting the door slam behind her, Melinda blurted out, "You got your dream!"

After I left for Alaska, Melinda drove with Evan south to spend Christmas with his grandparents who lived just down the highway from Mount Bachelor in Bend, Oregon. A few weeks after the New Year, when the house on Little Rabbit Creek was furnished and Evan's new bedroom was ready for him, she put him on an Alaska Airlines flight to Anchorage. He began the second half of his sixth-grade education at Bear Valley Elementary, a spruce-forested quarter mile walk up the creek from the house.

As a loner-romanticist, being by myself that Christmas was no problem. I adored the idea of having another chance to travel the Inside Passage to Alaska. I knew that the ship would traverse the treacherous Wrangell Narrows, dubbed "Christmas Tree Alley" because of the flashing red and green lights on its dozens of navigational buoys lining the tightly twisting channel. Around midnight, I would be on deck below the wheelhouse, certainly alone, bundled up because of the sleet and snow, singing Christmas carols into the wind.

On a dark Saturday afternoon, the ferry made a four-hour stop in Wrangell to wait for the slack tide that provided safe passage through the Narrows. I grabbed my boarding pass and walked up the ramp and across the ferry terminal to the quaint Southeast Alaska-style home of Todd and Elsie Harding. I was to be their guest for Christmas Eve dinner. Todd ran jet boat tours on the Stikine River, and he had once taken Evan and me upriver to jump icebergs on the lake fed by Chief Shakes Glacier. We had finished the trip warming up from the typically drizzly day in the almost too-hot waters of the gigantic cedar tub at Chief Shakes Hot Springs.

After that dinner, the MS Matanuska continued north and docked in Haines on Monday evening. I drove off into the snowy darkness in the Sidekick, and the town rapidly receded in my rear-view mirror. I was heading out of town along the Chilkat River toward a remote border station in the corner of northwest British Columbia. Would Canada Customs be open on the night before Canadian Boxing Day? I was relieved when I saw a few other vehicles, mostly Canadian citizens, also in line. I recognized them from the Matanuska as the people I had met on their way home to Whitehorse, Yukon Territory.

The customs officers poked through my belongings, and I presented proof of my new job in Alaska. With no hiccups at the border, I soon found myself driving in 10 inches of fresh snow, my headlights illuminating the snowbanks and hills as I ascended from coastal Alaska to Haines Junction, Yukon. Though I arrived to find a motel displaying a "vacancy" sign, a hot meal was out of the question; no restaurants would be open that night or the next morning. Fortunately, the room was warm.

Starting well before sunrise the next morning, on a day that would only briefly see daylight, I found a gas station where I could get coffee and junk food. Somewhat recharged, I headed up the Alaska Highway toward the border where I would cross back into the United States. It was cloudless, and billions of Milky Way stars silhouetted the peaks of Canada's Kluane National Park. There were no oncoming headlights on the road. The air temperature was about 15 below zero Fahrenheit, which made for quiet driving over the ice, which becomes far less slippery at extreme low temperatures. The few instances when I needed to pee, I simply pulled to a stop, turned off the headlights, and did my business in the middle of the highway. Each time, I walked a short distance from the purr of the car's engine to take in the grandeur of the subarctic mountains. There was no thought of turning off the vehicle; that would be foolhardy at the end of December in the Far North. I experienced the sensation of being totally alone in nature, yet not feeling lonely. When my reverie was finally overcome by the bitter cold, I would get back in the warm car—the heater stayed on "high" for the entire journey. Even so, I ended up needing to wrap my extra jacket around my left leg next to the cold door to keep warm.

After Beaver Creek, Yukon, I reached United States Customs, and just beyond, the town of Tok, Alaska. I began seeing the occasional vehicle on the roadway as I passed over Mentasta Summit toward a comfortable night in a motel in Glennallen and a big breakfast the following morning. The final day of the journey was to continue on the Glenn Highway—over the pass, down to Chickaloon and Palmer, and finally into Anchorage. At a combination truck stop/motel on Eureka Summit, the high point of the Glenn Highway, a trucker noticed I was headed toward Anchorage. He cautioned me that a warm front was coming in off Cook Inlet and that the road was soon to become extremely slick.

I had been gingerly creeping in the darkness along the curves of the highway for a half hour out of Eureka when I came upon a light-show of flares and flashing lights and slid to a stop. It turned out that a 20-something male driver had skidded into the rocks on the side of a canyon, flipped his pickup truck onto its top, and slid into the opposite guard rail. His vehicle had managed to roll back onto its wheels, but the truck's canopy and its contents had been catapulted over the guard rail and into the abyss below. Two big-rig truckers who had been traveling in tandem as a safety precaution had radioed the Alaska State Troopers, who in turn dispatched a wrecker from Palmer. The highway was blocked in both directions, but that was mostly irrelevant, as only a few truckers and the odd traveler like me were out that day.

The flares and flashing lights reflected off the icy roadway, and the pickup driver moved to the warmth of the Trooper's cruiser. The tow-truck driver grinned as he skated comically across the road, doing performance art for my benefit in the Suzuki's headlights, on his way to cinch up the wreck for the haul back to Palmer.

Two hours after the road re-opened, I was cruising through Palmer below the dramatic vista of Pioneer Peak on the now four-lane continuation of the Glenn Highway. Coming into Anchorage, I drove through the heart of downtown and across the city, then up Rabbit Creek Road to my house on Snowflake Drive. That night, I'd be camping on the master bedroom carpet. I had ordered a mattress from JC Penney, and it was scheduled to be delivered the following afternoon. It would be a couple weeks before the bed frame and my other furniture would arrive, but all I could think about was how glad I was to be home, and how a lifelong dream was finally coming true.

The next morning, I showered and shaved and reported to the office for my first day of work. I was thankful for a breakfast of doughnuts and coffee in the break room. My office was beautifully functional, and my new coworkers heartily welcomed me. I snapped a photo showing my new desk and the view of the Chugach Mountains bordering the city. I sent the picture and my warm greetings to my PEMCO friends back in Seattle where I had served the muktuk—ending one journey and starting another.

2

Piss Omelet

Tourists come to Alaska to see the state with North America's highest mountains, 3 million lakes, 46,600 miles of coastal shoreline, and 56 million acres of national parks. I felt I had won life's lottery when I landed a job that would take me from Ketchikan to Utkiaġvik, and from Northway to Unalaska.

An early example of the type of insurance claims I handled was the case of a kindly grandma from Oregon. She broke her hip when a boardwalk constructed over some tide pools at a wilderness lodge collapsed. She was in good spirits at the hospital, despite having undergone emergency surgery. Her only regret was that she had been sedated and slept through the first helicopter and private jet ride of her life.

Even though she explained that she wasn't interested in suing anyone, she would need more help with her considerable medical bills and a medical-evacuation flight back to Portland, and then to Eugene, Oregon. The site of the accident was on a remote island in Prince William Sound, and I needed to snap photos and take measurements of the failed boardwalk, as well as get eyewitnesses statements from staff members. It was short-sleeve weather under blue skies in the second week of September when I flew to Valdez and then boarded the same tour boat the woman had taken, the only practical way to reach the island. We navigated among icebergs at the Columbia Glacier, and we saw seals, otters, and whales, along with shorebirds and the parrots of the North, orange-billed tufted puffins.

When at last the boat stopped at the lodge, I skipped the buffet and immediately got to work. I shimmied around the barricade on the collapsed boardwalk to take photos and measurements. When I interviewed the few staff members that witnessed the collapse, I reached a simple verdict: the collapse had happened due to rusted out steel brackets that a biannual inspection should have detected. I ended up doing roughly three hours of bona fide work. Shortly after I finished my investigation, the boat tour was departing. I had missed the wood smoked salmon buffet, but on board I would settle for crab cakes and battered halibut.

In addition to raw physical beauty, another silver lining of my job came in the form of assignments taking me to parts of Alaska where tourism was still mostly a foreign concept. I'd bring my sleeping bag and carry easy-to-pack snacks like beef jerky and Pringles. Insulated boots and a heavy parka were essential most of the year. When my assignments were in Western Alaska, I often flew on Alaska Airlines to Bethel, the dominant hub of Western Alaska. From there, you could board a single engine aircraft to take you an hour or two further into the vast wetland environment.

By jet, Bethel lies an hour and ten minutes west of Anchorage and has about 6,500 residents. From there, one can reach 56 Yup'ik and Cup'ik Eskimo villages on rivers, seashores, and lakes spanning a region larger than the state of Ohio. The traditional Yup'ik name for the area that later became Bethel is *Mamterilleq*, "place of many caches." As a language nerd, my interest in this region was originally piqued by a BBC broadcast carried on Alaska Public Radio that explained that Yup'ik had the most sophisticated grammar of any language the investigative team had ever studied.

Moravian missionaries, from what is now eastern Germany, settled along this part of the Kuskokwim

River nearly two centuries ago. They dubbed their settlement Bethel, meaning "house of God" in the language of the Old Testament. Unlike other missionary groups that came into Alaska after its purchase from Russia in 1867, the Moravians sought to understand, rather than eliminate Native ways, and their scholars established the Yup'ik language's orthography and produced its first grammar. They translated the New Testament and other books into Yup'ik. Their work ultimately became the foundation of the Yup'ik language curriculum that the University of Alaska Fairbanks teaches today.

BET is the three-letter airline code for the Bethel Airport. Because the region's tundra is underlain by permafrost, seasonal melting and upwelling below the surface lends a rollercoaster-like quality to the asphalt on the city's sole highway. The only time this is not the case is when the state transportation department wages its war on the frost heaves and smooths things out every few years. At the first turn in the highway, there is a sign welcoming visitors to Mamtcrilleq, and underneath it reads: "*Paris on the Kuskokwim.*" This route into town is called the Chief Eddie Hoffman Highway, and it leads to a three-way intersection with Ridgecrest and Main, streets that many consider to be the center of town. However, given the myriad lakes and bogs in the area and the roadways that twist and turn unpredictably, a map of Bethel gives one the impression that city planners were having a squirt gun fight with ink.

There are no roads to or from Bethel, and any food that can't be hunted, fished, or grown, arrives by air or barge. When the Kuskokwim River is free of ice, vessels from Seattle bring heavy equipment and building materials, but for the rest of the year, big-ticket items such as new cars are flown in, adding thousands of dollars to the price tag. Overall, the cost of living is exorbitant.

At 702 miles long, the Kuskokwim River and its nearby big sister, the Yukon, 1,982 miles in length, are as mighty as the grand region they define. The whole area—encompassing more than 50,000 square miles—is called the Yukon-Kuskokwim Delta. Its waterways transport people in boats over vast distances, and after the ice becomes thick enough in the winter months, the river opens for snowmachines (Alaskan for "snowmobiles"), cars and trucks and, of course, dogsleds. Bethel is historically Yup'ik Eskimo. The Yup'ik language, or Yugtun, is alive and spoken by thousands. It appears on broadcasts of the local public radio station, KYUK, and it drives the city's impressive immersion school, *Ayaprun Elitnaurvik*.

Yup'ik friends made in Bethel can easily become friends for life, but this city, which attracts blue-collar workers from Southern states such as Alabama and Louisiana, harbors ugly racism, too. Though the Yup'ik people have lived here for at least 10,000 years according to archeologists, some White newcomers have the tendency to act as if they have proprietary rights.

During the 1992 Rodney King riots in Los Angeles, thousands of residents of the neighborhood known as Korea Town were burned out of their homes and businesses. A great many fled, and a portion of those ended up in Bethel, just about as far away in miles and culture as you can get from Los Angeles and still be in the United States. Korean arrivals to Bethel spiked in the early 1990's, and Korean entrepreneurs opened restaurants, hair salons, and toy stores, while a great many drove taxis.

With less than 45 miles of roads, including every side street inside town, and essentially nowhere to go, few people in Bethel own cars. People get around town on foot, on snowmachines, on four-wheelers, or by bicycle. A more comfortable option is a taxi, but unlike in the Lower 48, Bethel taxis don't necessarily take you from points A to B. They are shared taxis, and depending on your luck, you may end up on a very roundabout route to your destination.

As a casualty claims adjuster, I came face to face with animosity toward Koreans in Bethel time and again. One prime example was a rear-end collision on the Chief Eddie Hoffman Highway at the intersection with

Akiak Drive, kitty-corner from the police station. A Korean taxi driver coming into town from the airport signaled for a left turn onto Akiak Drive and stopped because of an oncoming car. Another taxi, not driven by a Korean, had been following too closely. The rear taxi struck the Korean taxi so hard that it ricocheted across the ice onto Akiak. A Bethel Police officer heard the crash from inside the station and ran outside to set out flares. Miraculously, nobody was seriously injured, but both taxis had to be towed from the scene.

It is elementary traffic law that in a rear-end collision, the driver who runs into a stopped vehicle that has properly signaled for a legal left turn is at fault. However, these rules did not appear to apply in Bethel at the time. For when I picked up the police report, I discovered that the Korean driver had been ticketed for "improper stopping." The fact that this wasn't a legitimate traffic violation in Alaska didn't matter. There was nothing that I as an adjuster could do. In similar cases that followed, I started calling that type of ticket a "DWK," *Driving While Korean*. Fortunately, after too many years of such nonsense, the Alaska State Troopers seized control of the Bethel Police Department. After instituting key reforms, including firing a handful of officers and requiring special ethics training, the Troopers returned management to the City of Bethel in 2003.

The long sub-Arctic summer days in Bethel are marked by the presence of a rich variety of migratory birds, which come to feast on the mosquitoes and other insects on the dozens of lakes in and around town. Mosquitoes find human victims by following their exhaled carbon-dioxide, and one upside of the often-breezy conditions in Bethel is that one's breath gets carried away with the wind before these bloodthirsty pests can find their marks. Despite inconveniences like these, in summer or winter the tundra is a place to appreciate nature's peace and grandeur.

In June 2002, as was typical for an assignment in Bethel, I had multiple claim files in my briefcase. The most straightforward of my assignments that day was a simple fender bender at the entrance to the Swanson's grocery and hardware stores. A roofer from the Lower 48 was backing up in a rusty pickup. The side mirrors were long gone, and the canopy had a sheet of plywood where the rear window should have been. He had backed up smack-dab into the passenger side of a Korean-driven taxi, which a few minutes before had pulled up to the loading zone in front of Swanson's.

I met the pickup truck's middle-aged owner in front of the store. He had gone to the taxi company's insurance agent in town to file a claim for the damage to his pickup. In turn, the Omaha-based insurer directed me to investigate. I conducted a recorded interview to get the driver's version of the accident. Then I photographed and measured the damage to the pickup, which amounted to a now missing rear bumper and a large dent in the tailgate.

That same afternoon, I met with the Korean taxi driver. His English was limited, so I retrieved two Matchbox toy cars from my briefcase that I kept for these situations. I drew a diagram of the parking area in front of Swanson's and asked him to show me what happened. I also shot photos of the damage to his taxi and instructed him to get a repair estimate from one of the body shops in town. He needed the repairs done fast, given that the cab was his main source of income.

Both drivers agreed on the facts. The fellow in the pickup had just returned to his truck after shopping. He had parked with his front bumper facing the building in the space closest to the front door. After coaxing the reluctant engine to life, he wasted no time in backing up. In the meantime, the Korean taxi driver had pulled up and dropped off two ladies, who went inside the store. Then Bam! The pickup's rear bumper bashed into both of the taxi's passenger-side doors. The driver of the pickup emerged screaming. When the taxi driver didn't understand him, he yelled even louder.

After a day of work in which the Swanson's accident was only one of several investigations, I secured my briefcase and headed over to the home Jim and Norma

Wyckoff in the "Blueberry Sub" for an always lovely dinner, before returning my rental car and catching the evening jet back to Anchorage. Norma, who then worked at Malone and Company, the insurance agent for most of Bethel's taxis, helped me every time I flew to Bethel by providing a back office where I could interview drivers, witnesses, and bodily injury claimants. Especially when the temperature on the street was minus 30 F, I don't know how I could have done my job without that workspace.

Back in Anchorage, it was my job to distill the recorded interview and photos into a report for the insurance company in Nebraska. In my documentation of the accident, I included the fact that the pickup driver had told me he knew that taxis stopped at the front door of Swanson's many times a day. He had insisted, however, that this Korean cab driver was like all the others, irresponsible and happy to park behind other vehicles as a ploy to collect insurance money. I might have felt a little sorry for the outcome of my investigation if not for his "I'm White, I'm right" attitude. I sent my comprehensive report to Omaha, and after conferring with the company, I called the pickup driver on his work phone.

I gave him the verdict: You were solely responsible for this accident. You backed your pickup into a stopped vehicle that was in a designated spot for loading and unloading passengers. Moreover, you couldn't see what was behind you because you had no side mirrors and the rear-view mirror was blocked by a sheet of plywood. The insurance company will not pay for your damage. Instead, you will have to pay to repair the taxi. You told me that you have no liability insurance, so you will have to pay out of pocket. The taxi's insurance company will pay for the cab's damage using his "uninsured motorist property damage liability coverage" (UM-PD). Then the company will bill you for what they paid. If you are unable to pay, you will be reported to the Alaska Division of Motor Vehicles, and your license will be suspended. If you don't repay the damage, then your annual Permanent Fund Dividend check will be garnished until you have paid what you owe.

The fellow fired off a string of expletives about "them damn Koreans" and hung up. I had already explained to him that written confirmation of everything would arrive in the mail. At that point, I sent my file to the insurance company's UM-PD unit for the taxi's repair, and then to the insurance company's subrogation (collections) unit. For me, the claim was a wrap.

I was in Bethel often. Six months after the Swanson's investigation, my Alaska Airlines jet arrived in the dark at 7:30 AM, with the temperature at 26 degrees below zero. Bethel's only car rental outfit opened at 9 AM, and I had reserved one of their five cars. Fortunately, they kept them in a heated garage, so I knew that mine would start, and that I probably wouldn't be shutting off the engine all day. I hadn't eaten before flying out because I had planned to go to a cozy spot called Diane's Restaurant to have breakfast and wait for the car rental agency to open.

A taxi dropped me off in front of the restaurant on a clear winter morning with a crescent moon and a dome of stars. I knocked the snow off my boots on the steel-grate stairs. I could see into the kitchen from where I stepped inside the arctic entry and took off my parka. I happened to make eye contact with the cook. I recognized him from somewhere, but I couldn't recall where. I could tell that he also recognized me. I didn't think much of it.

There were people seated at two other tables in the dining room. A waitress in jeans and a sweatshirt brought me coffee, orange juice, and toast. About 10 minutes later, she brought me the cheese omelet I had ordered, and she refilled my coffee mug. I thanked her and spooned some salsa from a jar in the middle of the table onto the omelet. It looked good, so I carved out a big chunk with my fork and guided it into my mouth. The texture was what I had expected, but the taste was instantly reminiscent of the smell of a gas station's urinal. It was too late to spit out the chunk, so I grabbed the orange juice and tried to wash away the taste that caused me to convulse. As I pushed the plate to the other side of the table, I suddenly recalled that the cook was the driver of that rusty, brown pickup six months earlier.

I sat still for a moment while my pulse returned to normal. What should I do? The fellow was looking for a reaction, so I decided that I would act as if nothing had happened. The lack of a response would convince him that I was dumber than he already thought. No matter, I could understand the guy's anger; it would not help matters if he lost his job. Furthermore, neither the waitress nor Diane had anything to do with it, so I didn't want to cause them any grief.

I ate the rest of the toast with jelly, finished my orange juice and coffee, and then I just left a tip like usual. At the counter I asked the waitress to call me a taxi to take me to the rental car agency. I'd be early, but they had chairs inside where I could wait until the office opened. When I got out of the second taxi of the morning and walked through the snow to Emerald Car Rentals, the saga of the piss omelet had already left my mind. The orange glow over the tundra to the southeast meant the sun would be coming up in a couple hours. It was going to be a quintessentially perfect Western Alaska winter day in Paris on the Kuskokwim.

Part Two

Young First-Responder

The chapters in this section flash back to experiences from my youth that eventually invited me to deal with people in crisis in the mountain wilderness.

The bliss of the ascent in the icy wilderness.

3

I'll Do the Opposite

"Bedazzled" is the word I would use to describe my childhood relationship to wilderness mountains. At Mount Rainier National Park, I was treated to the annual Longmire Picnic, an event where the progeny of this Pacific Northwest pioneer family reunited to celebrate their heritage. Logically, it was held in the campground and meeting hall at Longmire, the park's headquarters. My mother was born Thelma Longmire, and my aunts, uncles, and cousins shared that birth name; so that's how I came to be a part of this affair.

Usually, after some fried chicken and potato salad, I didn't stick around for the speeches at the annual gathering. Instead, I bushwhacked my way over to the hell-roaring summertime glacier-melt of the Nisqually River. I sat awestruck astride a boulder on the shore and listened to other Volkswagen-size rocks tumble along the riverbed in the frothy, gray torrent flowing to Puget Sound. I knew, because my great uncle Len Longmire had been the first guide on Mount Rainier, that attaining the squinting-bright whiteness of the summit above me was possible. I wondered if I would grow up enough to go up there myself someday.

In kindergarten, the adults said my Crayola stick figures were artistic. I sketched, painted, and crafted mosaics of peaks and glaciers. After a family hike to Boulder Lake at the base of Boulder Peak near Olympic Hot Springs, Mom told me she knew I was hooked on mountains. She had seen this type of enchantment in her Longmire uncles of Mount Rainier fame. After Boulder Peak, she put me in touch with some adult friends in the Seattle-based climbing club, the *Mountaineers*. They in turn encouraged me to apply for early admission to the "Basic Climbing Course." I remembered what Mom had said with a sigh: "*It gets in your blood.*" I didn't respond, but I could have told her that I was already convinced of that fact.

In the following years, I was to learn that people pursuing their mountain-passion sometimes fall and bleed, and that the experience of coming to the aid of these people can be superbly rewarding. Occasionally, an injured climber doesn't make it, but even then, you draw strength from knowing that you did the best you could.

At Mercer Island Junior High School in 1960, a low-budget documentary film influenced me beyond any other movie I had ever seen. Before the lights went down and the projector started humming, I listened to a man named Jim Whittaker speak to the junior high ski club about responsible comportment in the mountains. Whittaker, along with his twin Lou and another climbing legend, Ome Daiber, had produced the movie, *Mountains Don't Care, But We Do*. These fellows were not just the producers, but along with various conscripts from the *Mountaineers*, founded in 1906, an organization dedicated not just to climbing and hiking, but also outdoor education and preservation of the vanishing wilderness. This epic performance inaugurated the 'Seattle Mountain Rescue Council," an organization that would go on to become a model for other volunteer rescue organizations in the mountains of the American West.

Just six years later, during summers away from college, Jim Whittaker ended up being my boss after I landed a job at REI. Back then, it was just called the

"Co-Op," as Lloyd and Mary Anderson and several other Seattle climbers had originally organized it as a cooperative to bring in strong, hickory-shaft-ice-axes, Mammut climbing ropes, and forged pitons from Austria and Switzerland.

In 1963, Jim was the first American to climb Mount Everest during an era when it took mettle and stamina to reach one of the fourteen 8,000-meter summits in the world; unlike today, when all you need is to be in good physical shape and have a huge bank account. Today, sixty-thousand dollars will buy you the gear, permits, airfare, hotels, and Sherpa guides to join the crowd and help you avoid the frozen-in-place corpses of other climbers, so that you can get hauled to the top of Everest.

Among Jim Whittaker's many other accomplishments, in 1965, he led Robert F. Kennedy to the summit of Mount Kennedy, a major summit in Yukon's Kluane Lake National Park. The Canadian Parliament had just named Mount Kennedy in honor of Robert's brother John Fitzgerald Kennedy, who had been assassinated in November 1963. In the joy felt by both men who had become joined in mountaineering camaraderie on that expedition, Jim could not have possibly seen into the future. Robert Kennedy would also meet the same fate of being assassinated several years later.

On June 6, 1968, I was eating dinner with German friends in a little lodge in the mountains of the Berner Oberland in Switzerland when a staticky transistor radio brought the news that U.S. presidential candidate Robert Kennedy had died of multiple gunshot wounds. A couple fellows sitting across the wooden table from me saw that I turned pale. They asked if I was okay, and I told them to just give me a moment, and I'd be fine. I wasn't fine. However, my grief was nothing compared to Jim's. A Co-Op mail-order-packing friend that I had worked with in Seattle let me know by letter how profoundly affected Jim was. He went back to Washington, D.C., to be a pallbearer, proving once again that Whittaker was not just tall, but a giant among men.

My own memories of Jim's days at the Co-Op are more prosaic. He was the sales floor manager, and from time to time he asked me to single-handedly manage the afternoon to closing shift in the original Pike Street store, in the heart of downtown Seattle. In the early days, folks called REI the "*Mountaineers Co-Op*" because it was located across the hall from the *Mountaineers* Club Room on the upper floor of a building, over a jewelry store and a dive bar. Working there by myself was quiet but fun, and a decent day's receipts at the little downtown store totaled around $200. Today, REI's gross annual revenue is shy of four billion dollars.

Jim offered me the job of managing the new Berkeley, California, branch store, the first expansion outside of Seattle. I told him that I was sorry, because in a couple months I would be leaving for university in Germany. Wally Smith, one of my two sales floor buddies then, accepted the job and went to Berkeley. Wally became the CEO of REI, while Dennis Madsen, the other sales floor friend and co-worker, became to CFO. Do I regret turning Jim down that day? Considering the adventures and misadventures that my life has given me since, the answer is no.

I chuckle when I remember the times Jim would occasionally break into salsa dance moves when business was slow at the Eleventh Avenue store. I also recall the time a woman came in and wanted the tall, handsome, and famous Jim Whittaker to personally sell her whatever climbing boots he recommended. When it came time for her to sit down and take off her shoes and socks, however, Jim slipped away and told me to take over. That was the first and only time in my life that a woman was disappointed to have me touch her feet. Over the years, I had gained a reputation among my female friends as someone who gave good foot massages. In my freshman year at PLU, a nursing student studying massage therapy taught me how to do it. I live in Alaska today, but some women up here still shuck off their boots and ask for a foot massage, and I am happy to oblige.

Regarding my summer co-workers at REI who were awarded opportunities for promotion, Wally Smith became CEO and Dennis Madsen became CFO. Dennis used to mock me by calling me "Flash" whenever my pace suddenly slowed while gathering the deadly-dull mail orders. In later years, Dennis occasionally dropped by PEMCO to pick me up and take me out to lunch in his European sports car.

When REI was searching for a location to build their new Seattle flagship store, they chose 222 Yale Avenue North, a site immediately to the south of the PEMCO building. As it happened, my desk faced the third-floor windows overlooking first the demolition of an old industrial building, and then the excavation for the new superstore and its underground parking garage. I was a daily spectator of the construction project and the racket it created.

In 1994, PEMCO President Stanley O. McNaughton decided it would be a neighborly thing to organize a luncheon and tour of our facilities to welcome REI to the neighborhood. After some speeches, the group guided Wally Smith on a tour of the PEMCO complex. The day before, Human Resources had sent a memo alerting all the staff that an entourage of board members would be bringing a VIP through the building. We lowly employees were instructed to work uninterrupted and to refrain from speaking to the group.

It was natural that the entourage would make their way to the windows overlooking the REI construction site, and the most unobstructed view in the building was from the windows near my desk. Wally saw me at my desk and said, "Hi, Kristian, I knew you worked here. We've known each other for a long time, haven't we?" I stood up to shake his hand, and behind Wally I noted the corporate warriors in dark suits glowering at me for having the audacity to get out of my chair. Wally then sat down on the corner of my desk, and we chatted for several minutes. The stern fellows standing behind Wally had no choice but to wait for him to be done.

The next day at work, the fact that the CEO of REI had taken a seat on my desk was a hot topic. Charlie Theaker, a friend and star litigator in the Legal Department, already knew my story of how I had turned down the opportunity that could well have made me that very VIP. He quipped, "Kristian, I am thinking about buying [such and such] stock. I want to know what you think because whatever you say, I'll do the opposite."

4

It Gets in Your Blood

At 4:30 AM on a Saturday in April 1962, the Cascades were emerging in shades of orange and pink on the eastern horizon. My father dropped me off at a *Mountaineers* ride-share meeting spot in Seattle. I hefted my pack onto my shoulders with a groan, and my dad said, "If I tried to make you carry all that stuff, you'd throw a fit." How could I explain to Dad the thing that Mom observed years before? This isn't like mowing the lawn or hauling tanks of gas to the water ski boat. The love of mountains was in my blood.

I was just 14, and we lived in a house with 180 feet of waterfront on Pine Lake near Issaquah, Washington, which in those days was far from the city in rural King County. I thanked him for driving me all the way from Issaquah, across Mercer Island, and over the floating bridge into Seattle. I explained that I had arranged a ride all the way back to the house that night and not to worry; I'd probably be late. That was the first time I told my parents that I was headed into the mountains but not to worry, something that I would repeat time and again in the following years.

Eleven hours after I said goodbye to Dad, I was standing on a two-foot-wide ledge on a Class 4 rock cliff. I unclipped my aluminum carabiner rappel device from the climbing rope and hooked it out of the way onto the waist-loop of my seat harness. Now, it was my turn to climb back up the same rock face I had trusted in my gear to descend. I reached with my left hand to grab the first handhold, and at the same time I shouted up to my out-of-sight friend Pete, "Climbing!" I heard him yell back, "Climb!"

Pete was taking up the slack in the rope as I moved slowly upward, executing an anchored sitting-belay, meaning, in an instant he would wrap the rope around his torso to stop me if he heard me yell "Falling!" or if the rope just started zinging through his hands. I emerged up over the edge of the rock platform and grinned at Pete. "Off Belay!" I yelled, and he responded in kind with, "Belay Off."

Both Peter and I were students in the *Mountaineers'* Basic Climbing Course, which had started in January that year. Our textbook was the first edition of *Mountaineering: The Freedom of the Hills*. (Today this tome is in its 10th edition.) Our training was being held at Mount Erie on Fidalgo Island, a mountain climbers' playpen due to the fact it remained snow-free when the Cascades and Olympics were still buried under 10 feet of white. Erie's vertical escarpments have more than 400 named routes varying in difficulty, from hands-and-feet scrambling to Class 4 through Class 6 climbing, calling for rope anchors and belaying. On Erie, there are even a couple overhangs for the stupendously fit and skilled to prove that Spiderman has nothing on them; but the back side of Erie is just a pleasant hike up through the forest to the top.

Erie offers over-wintered climbers a way out of hibernation, and a way to work off some flab while honing their skills. It also gave newbies like Pete and me a place to learn the fundamentals. This was the first rock-climbing field trip of the Basic Climbing Course, and only about a quarter of those who paid the tuition in January would complete the lectures, attend the practices, participate in the field trips (such as Erie), and knock off the required "experience climbs" in order to graduate in October.

The minimum age for the course was 18, but the *Mountaineers* Climbing Committee would admit applicants as young as us two buddies, age 14, if adult climbers could be found to vouch for them on a form. Including Pete and me, there were a total of eight teens who entered the course in 1962, and we were required to recite by rote the *Mountaineers' Climbing Code* on page 264 of *Freedom of the Hills*. Of the eight commandments contained in this directive, one was, "Judgment shall not be swayed by desire when choosing the route or deciding to turn back," a principle I later realized would have served me well throughout my life if I had paid better attention to it.

On Erie, the instructors reinforced what we'd been taught about belays, anchor placement, balance climbing, and the *pièce de résistance,* rappelling. The first time I stepped backwards off a cliff-face and waited for the rope to stretch until the anchor took hold, my brain screamed to me, "Stop this, you idiot. We're gonna die!" I tried to reason with that panicked voice inside me, "You've practiced this before. You'll be fine."

On the ledge I had reached climbing up the cliff face, I was standing near Pete, who was still seated. I went into my pack for some snacks, and he unhooked from his belay anchor and came over to stand beside me. I didn't get a chance to ask if he wanted some M&Ms before shouts came from above, "Rock! Rock! Rock!" A climber had dislodged a hand-grenade-size piece of Mount Erie. This mountain is mostly composed of feldspar-diorite, which doesn't break off easily, but every mountain—from the weakest basalt to the mightiest granite—is under the dictates of gravity.

I scanned the cliffs above to see where the rock might be. We'd been taught to remain calm, and that you won't know until the last seconds whether to stay put or get out of the way. Both Pete and I were wearing new REI rock helmets, but as good as they were, they could not shield our faces from a projectile ricocheting off the rocks at an oblique angle. Suddenly, Bullseye! Pete was struck between the eyes. Blood gushed. I grabbed for my first aid kit for gauze to staunch the flow.

Several minutes later, two instructors descended from above. Pete had remained conscious, and his pupils were normal. He answered their questions, as they tried to determine whether he had sustained a concussion. They bandaged him further and determined that he could be "walked out." That would be far better than getting a stretcher up there, which would mean an exit off the mountain would be made in the middle of the night. One big guy hefted Pete's backpack on top of his own, and then as an afterthought before they both departed, he asked if I'd be okay by myself. Sure! I affirmed. (Pete ended up in the Anacortes hospital emergency room, where he was treated and released. Someone drove him to his home on Mercer Island. I never heard how his mom reacted to seeing his bandaged-up visage that night.)

I remained on the mountain, alone. Cloudless sky, no breeze. No reason to rush. I swigged some water to wash down the last of my M&Ms. My fingertips were reddened and appeared to be missing layers of skin. The rocks of Mount Erie had begun the process of turning my kid's hands into the callused hands of a climber. I admired the courageous single flowers that adorned cracks in the rock around me. I scanned the purple and white summits to the west, comprising the front range of the Olympics within the national park. Below my perch were viridian islets seemingly swimming on a cerulean sea. This was the grand inland waterway that Captain George Vancouver named *Puget's Sound* after his lieutenant Peter Puget in 1792.

Below my perch, there were also seemingly endless forests of Douglas fir, cedar, and hemlock. As I looked at the verdure, I remembered the breakfast table at home where Mom left a copy of the *Ladies' Home Journal*. It had been laid open to an article where a fashion designer stated that green should not be paired with blue. But from my vantage point, everything I could see below was blue on green and green on blue. Apparently, God didn't read women's magazines.

The sun-warmed air carried the fragrance of firs, lichen on rock, slide alder, cranberry brush, dogwood, and purple lupine. After a day that had required the young adrenal glands atop my kidneys to squirt their stuff into my blood again and again, I was now in the endorphin-laden afterglow. I wondered if the winged and four-legged critters up here could be as intoxicated with the glories of the mountains as I was in that moment.

Twenty years later, I found an answer—albeit in a quite different way—on a slope below Yakima Peak inside Mount Rainier National Park. The first freeze and snow of October that year had covered the previous summer's blueberry bonanza. Then two weeks after the hard freeze, it warmed again for two weeks. In the Alps of Bavaria, they call this phenomenon *Altweibersommer* (old wives' summer). At the foot of Mount Rainier, it had warmed the fruit, turning everything into a natural winery, with each bulging berry becoming a sort of tiny wine flask. Varied Thrushes and Gray Jays had flocked in to quaff the booze. They were singing the mating songs of spring as they soared and then dove again, often missing their intended landing spots and tumbling tail over beak. They rested, fluffed their feathers—regained some dignity—and then gobbled more berries. I wondered to myself how thrushes and jays sleep off a hangover.

Returning to the 14th year of my life and the Basic Climbing Course, I signed up to take on Mount

Saint Helens as my first experience climb, ascending features that would be exploded into the sky in the 1980 eruption. In my search through Dad's closet for climbing trousers, I happened upon the Filsons that he was wearing in his honeymoon photo at Sol Duc Hot Springs in the Olympic Mountains. While Dad was in good physical shape, he wasn't as skinny as he used to be, so he let me have them.

On the Mount Saint Helens climb, there were a few open crevasses and a bunch of suspicious depressions we needed to jump across. This required rope team cooperation, with slack maintained in the climbing rope sufficient for jumping and not being pulled backward, potentially toward a hidden crevasse. A month earlier on Mount Rainier's Nisqually Glacier, I had rappelled into the fluorescent blue depths of crevasses. I was in awe of the aesthetic beauty then, but I had no desire to involuntarily plunge into one now.

When I reached the top of the 9,677-foot peak, I made my way across the crater to the geographic summit—a hurricane-wind-blasted hill of ice with a 360° view. Looking out from the spot, I had to agree with the mountain-climber poet who once christened the grand volcanoes of the Pacific Ring of Fire, volcanoes of which St. Helens is one, *Islands in the Sky*.

After tiring of struggling to stand upright in the wind, our rope team of three descended toward the Dog's Head route, and when at last the mountain's crevasses were above us, we unroped. Now free to move around, a couple thousand vertical feet of glissading (*glissade* means to slide on snow, usually on one's butt) awaited us. At first, the snow was cushiony-soft, but as I descended the mountain, the scruffy, bumpy ice numbed my hind-end so much that I couldn't feel it anymore. As it turned out, I didn't know that the snow lower on the mountain was inter-layered with shards of volcanic pumice and pieces of angular scoria. In my long glissade, I had pumiced the rear end off of Dad's Filsons, partially shredding my tightey-whitey Jockey shorts and fortunately running out of mountain before leaving what would have been a trail of blood.

On the climbers' trail back to the parking area, things warmed up (and by "things" I mean my derrière). I felt a breeze on my cheeks, and I don't mean the ones on my face. A young female climber came up behind me and apprised me of my situation. Mortified, I slipped off my parka and tied it around my waist; and it stayed there until I walked into my house on Pine Lake later that night.

I had just turned 15 when at around 2 PM on a July afternoon, a breeze on a blue-sky day wiped the sweat from my forehead. I unshouldered my pack and set it by my feet among the angular granodiorite slabs of the 7,835-foot summit of Sloan Peak, twelve miles southwest Glacier Peak. From our summit viewpoint, the whiteness of the 10,541-foot Glacier Peak stratovolcano reigned over the eastern horizon, while fifty other Cascades summits paid obeisance to her majesty.

On the Sloan climb, I found myself in the company of some Pacific Northwest mountaineering legends. As they ate their lunches, they named off dozens of the lesser peaks visible that diamond-bright afternoon. I was in wonderment. They told of bushwhacking on the Chilliwack near the Canadian border, establishing high camps on the super-glaciers in the Alaska Range, and summiting McKinley (it wouldn't be officially called "Denali" until 2015). I wondered, How could mere mortals know so much?

Sloan's alpine glaciers were relatively small. Even so, while plunge-stepping down, I broke through a chink in the roof of a hidden crevasse big enough to accommodate me and my entire rope team. I yelled "Falling!" but because I had been able to throw my body backwards away from the hole, their automatic dropping to the snow in ice-axe self-arrest position turned out to be just another practice session. I wiggled my way backwards and then peered into the abyss, shuddered a bit, and redirected my rope team to back up and detour around this trap.

Another glacier story came about 15 years later on Mount Baker. I was 30 years old, and had myself become a Basic Climbing Course instructor. It was late on a summer day, meaning the hard snow bridges of the morning had become soft and fragile. After summiting, we had broken high camp at the foot of volcanic spires opposite a feature known as the Roman Wall. During descents, it is easy to forget about inherent danger and become giddy with accomplishment. From the campsite on the glacier, it would only be another hour before we'd take off the crampons at the top of the lateral moraine called Heliotrope Ridge. Then, we'd hike the rest of the way, first on rocks and then on dirt trails, back to where the cars were parked.

After leaving camp, we resumed our positions, spread among four rope teams of three climbers each. I was in the middle spot on the first team. Before long, we were descending alongside a series of open fissures and junior seracs known as the "college crevasses," named in remembrance of students from Western Washington University who had perished there years earlier.

I noticed that 22-year-old Andy, at the head of my rope team, had gotten way too close to those crevasses. I yelled to him, "Stop! Hold it! You are too close and you have way too much rope out." The slope was steep, but he kept descending. "Did you hear me? Don't move! You've got too much slack." At last, he turned toward me, and I continued, "Do you see that monster hole to your right? It has an overhang, and you're on..." Andy was gone. I yelled, "Falling!" for him. I slammed my body into the glacier in the self-arrest position with the adze of my ice ax against my left shoulder, and I buried the pick as deep as I could into the ice below the soft surface. I saw nothing except the snow in front of my goggles. I waited 3 impossibly long seconds for the rope to go taut and start to drag me toward where Andy had disappeared. Fortunately, the woman behind me had kept the rope tight, and she, too, had immediately dropped into self-arrest when I yelled. When the rope finally became taut, we were pulled only about eight feet before stopping Andy's fall.

All of us assembled at the edge of the crevasse and worked together to bring Andy back up to the surface. When he emerged, his aluminum frame pack looked like a pretzel, but that was a good thing given it had served to break his fall. Except for a few bruises, he was okay. After packing away our crevasse rescue gear, we all regrouped into our original configuration to finish the descent. For the rest of the way down off the glacier, Andy kept the rope between him and me very tight.

After unroping on the rocks of Heliotrope Ridge, Andy hadn't even finished taking off his seat harness when he began to chatter about his thrill to be signed up for another experience climb the following weekend. It was obvious now. Climbing had gotten in his blood.

Sloan Peak in the Henry M. Jackson Wilderness, another later conservation victory adjacent to the Glacier Peak Wilderness

5

Basic Rock & Acid Rock

After Peter was clobbered between the eyes on Mount Erie, I knew that I wanted to become a wilderness first-responder. I had passed the American Red Cross standard first aid course, and the next step was the advanced program. In later years, my primary reference book became *Medicine for Mountaineering, Second Edition*. This manual, now in its seventh edition, is a field guide known around the world.

I cannot say that academics alone determined which university I would attend. By my senior year of high school, I already knew that I wanted to major in both German and philosophy, but I also knew I didn't want to go to the East Coast and leave the Cascades and the Olympics behind. Luckily, I found a place where the stars of academics and mountains aligned in Pacific Lutheran University. With its academic credentials born in the German Reformation, it was ideal for both language study and delving into the Western philosophy that arose out of ancient Greece. As my academic career blossomed, I also gave a nod to my naturalist tendencies by minoring in physical geology. As for the mountains side of the equation, the university was situated astride an escarpment on a glacial outwash plain below Mount Rainier, with the park's Nisqually Entrance just an hour away.

At PLU, I pushed the ski season on both ends, early in the fall and late in the spring. Saturdays were on the slopes, and Sundays were in the books. However, at times when the weather was crisp and the mountain dominated the view from campus, I faltered. My puke-green Studebaker station wagon still had shadows of government decals on its doors, because in its former life it had belonged to a ranger at Mount Rainier National Park. One Sunday, my car was calling, so I closed my books, grabbed my day pack and jogged to student parking. It seemed like the station wagon knew the way to the mountain on its own.

Reinhold Messner, a superhero South-Tyrolean mountain climber and world-famous author, wrote this question as a youngster, "*What is better? To sit in the pew on Sunday, unable to think about anything but the mountains, or to be in the mountains thinking about God?*" Messner may not have needed to worry about a Monday morning exam or have a paper due by noon like I did, but his sentiments expressed my feelings about priorities well.

I arrived back at the dorm late Sunday night; my roommate was already asleep. I tossed my pack on my bed and pulled the study curtain around my workspace. The desk light would suffice until dawn. My portable Royal typewriter, to which a technician had added German characters, was noisy, but my roommate didn't stir. Much later, I found out that because of my habits, he used earplugs. At 7:35 AM, I pulled the last sheet of paper out of the typewriter and headed to the Columbia Center cafeteria for coffee and a sweet roll on my way to class. In that dining hall, Rainier dominated the view through the enormous plate glass windows, and sipping my coffee, I paused again to study its glaciers in the morning light. Was it the caffeine or the view of the Mountain that jolted me to life? No matter, I'd sleep that afternoon.

As a PLU geology laboratory assistant, I helped students identify rocks and crystals and proctored their exams. In my dorm room I listened to Beethoven, Haydn, Schubert, Brahms, Mozart, and Heinrich Schütz on my stereo. Completing my junior year abroad at the University of Freiburg—where I became immersed in phenomenology, existentialism, the theories of essence and being, as well as the literally more down to earth subjects of the Upper Rhineland's Horst and Graben geology—I became even more out of touch with American pop culture than I had been before I left.

As for my fascination with geology, I knew that acidic rocks were generally crystalline, as well as the strongest and hardest. Among them were granite, schist, feldspar, gneiss, and diorite. On the other end of the chemical spectrum were the basic rocks, softer and more easily eroded than acidic rock. The grand volcanics, pyroclastics, and basalts of the Cascades were generally in this classification. But acidic characteristics carried over to the basic rock and vice versa, especially in examples of phenomenally beautiful metamorphosed rock. Even though I found acidic rocks to be more aesthetically pleasing, I adored the specimen walls of columnar basalt, as well as the outcroppings of pillow basalt in ancient outflows to the west of Rainier.

My second weekend back at PLU, immediately following the summer semester in Freiburg, I was invited to an off-campus party. Heavens! Why me? I stood around for a while, but then I overheard two freshman girls talking geology. One enthused to the other that she liked *soft rock, the basic stuff, more than the hard acid rock.* The other young lady countered, *No, hard rock is way more powerful; it's not quite as glaring, it has more substance.*

How in the name of Louis Agassiz did these girls just out of high school know this stuff? No matter, I saw now that my evening wasn't going to be boring after all. But how would I join their conversation? I would say that I overheard them, and that I was intrigued by gabbro, which can be the product of a molten union of acid and basic rock. The room was crowded, and I doubt the girls even noticed me standing there, but before I could open my mouth, they started naming bands and artists that played their favorite rock *music.* Oh, my. I slinked away and opened the sliding glass door to the porch; the cool air felt good on my red cheeks.

After PLU, I spent a summer of 1969 in the French part of Switzerland, taking courses at the University of Geneva, where I escaped to the Swiss and French Alps on weekends whenever I could. Then I entered graduate school as a teaching assistant in the German Department at the University of Washington. After that, I needed a job. My first gig was teaching German

101, 102, and 103 in the evening at Highline College in Des Moines, Washington. I soon learned that a perk of being an adjunct faculty member was that I could take one college course for free each quarter.

One evening when I checked in before my German class, there were boxes piled next to the administrative assistant's desk: bandages, slings, splints, plastic emergency airways, surgical tape, and rolls and rolls of gauze. I asked her what all this was for, and she responded that she had ordered everything off the manifest for the *Emergency Medical Technician* (EMT) training program, beginning in ten days. It was subsidized by King County for firefighters with the goal of promoting them from occasional first-responder duties to full-time EMT paramedic status.

Thinking that it was too much to hope for, I asked, "Would this course be open to me as adjunct faculty?" She said nobody on staff had ever asked this before, but to just wait and she'd see what the department head would say. Five minutes later she came back smiling broadly. "Yes, even though this is a contracted program, it was numbered and supervised as part of the college curriculum, so, yes, you are eligible. Let's get the enrollment forms started. You know, don't you, that everyone else in your program will be a fireman who has prior emergency first aid experience?" I nodded yes.

Fortunately, the German classes I taught didn't conflict with the EMT program. This schedule, however, meant that I spent every weekday evening at Highline, as well as some weekends doing practical field exercises. The first evening of class, I arrived early and chose a desk in the last row. A half-dozen other guys in their early twenties, just like me, were already there, congregating in the middle of the room. They were firefighters who had all worked together on a head-on collision the day before, in which both vehicles caught fire. They saw a torso separated from one of its arms. After extinguishing the flames, they used the Jaws of Life to reach two critically burned kids, pieces of skin peeling off, but still alive. The EMTs on scene took over and rushed them to Harborview Medical Center's burn unit in Seattle.

The guys in my classroom also discussed seeing brain matter on the upholstery of one of the cars. One of the obviously deceased fellows was missing most of his head; the firefighters were called back to the station before the skull could be located. While listening to these fellows, my stomach twisted into a knot. I asked myself if I was capable of handling this stuff. Then, as an official from King County's emergency services and a physician both stepped up to the podium, we all took our seats. They would be our team-teachers for the course. When I refocused my attention on them, I found my stomach stopped doing calisthenics.

Night by night, week by week, they regaled the class with melodramas, tragedies, and comedies, referring to what they called "combat emergency room medicine." The location to which an EMT delivers a patient is usually called the "emergency room," but it is more correctly called the "emergency department," for it is composed of numerous rooms, diagnostic equipment, and operating theaters. The most popular abbreviation used to be "the ED," but those two letters took a nosedive later when U.S. Senator and 1996 presidential candidate Bob Dole starting hawking Viagra on TV. He broke ground by telling America that he suffered from erectile dysfunction, and suddenly ED meant something else entirely.

The emergency physician teaching us explained that we would become accustomed to seeing naked people, such as burn victims and women and men fleeing sexual assault. He explained further that in serious accidents we would use our shears in counterintuitively delicate but quick cuts to remove clothing and determine the source of hemorrhages or find the origin of broken bones protruding through a shirt sleeve or a pant leg. In each case, it would be essential to identify ourselves to the victim and explain precisely what we were doing. While working, we'd ask questions such as "Where does it hurt the most?" Conversation helps in triage and also aids in determining the victim's level of both consciousness and sobriety. One or more of us would remain in the back of the aid vehicle all the way to the hospital, and we were to continue the conversation with the injured and thereby keep watch over their level of consciousness.

In the classroom unit on addressing the consequences of sexual violence, we learned that the improbability of scenarios would be surpassed by reality. Items such as a broken light bulb, a vodka bottle, a flashlight, and even a hockey stick might be found inserted into someone's genitourinary or anal openings, we were told. In most cases, as with other foreign objects, our job was not to remove it in the field unless a doctor on the radiophone told us to do so. We were to stabilize the injured and control bleeding. But never ever—even if we thought the victim was unconscious or dead—were we to express disdain, amazement, or revulsion at what we saw. That type of talk would have to wait until off-duty hours when we were far away. The physician said that he could not expect us to contain our astonishment at what we saw, but to just trust him. Over time the gruesome and the bizarre would need immediate attention but otherwise barely raise an eyebrow.

One Friday in the spring, our class at Highline was scheduled to report at 6 AM to the offices of the King County Medical Examiner, the morgue.

In 1973, the Medical Examiner was housed in the basement of what used to be the high school on top of Queen Anne Hill, an imposing structure of grand dimensions. This facility was a mere holding point until expanded facilities elsewhere in King County were authorized by the voters.

We Highline College EMT students, the class size now whittled down to about 12, were to be student-observers in a teaching autopsy. After registration at the administrative office, we took our places in a semi-circle below a cluster of surgical-theater lights. The floor was polished concrete. A staffer rolled in a stainless-steel gurney, similar to an operating table, but without any cushioning. It was slightly inclined with raised edges that funneled to a drain hole connected to a sewage link at the lower end. The lights went on, and lying before us was a naked, overweight male, balding, perhaps in his fifties.

The senior medical examiner walked in, gowned and gloved, holding a surgical mask in one hand. He took his place next to a table with his tools. They included scalpels, ordinary carpet knives, empty specimen jars, a hacksaw, an electric circular saw, and assorted sponges. The doctor welcomed us and made introductions, then he donned his mask and began.

Except for the fact that there were no bedclothes, the deceased looked like he was sleeping in the nude, aside from the tortuously-uncomfortable-looking wooden block that supported his head. My spot was adjacent to the deceased's left shoulder, which had a monstrous gash revealing a fractured humerus; the bone having evidently retreated inside the arm after tearing through the muscle and skin. The medical examiner told us that this gentleman had been brought in by an EMT ambulance after midnight. They didn't take him to a hospital because he was already in rigor mortis, and the doctor on duty had prepared the preliminary death certificate at the morgue. He chose this cadaver because the Seattle Police had called for a complete forensic evaluation to determine the cause of death, which was apparently something more than the shoulder injury.

Before doing any cutting, the doctor pointed out to the students that this body had no bruising on the chest and no evidence of cracked ribs from CPR (cardiopulmonary resuscitation). First-responders had recognized when they arrived that he was clearly deceased. Then he expressed frustration, "Why do I see so many frail elderly women and men with unnecessary broken ribs? Can't you EMT guys treat the dead with a bit more dignity?" His comment would take on irony over the next hours, during which no shortage of quips and gallows humor came out of his mouth.

His first action was to use a big carpet knife to rip a Y incision from below the nipples down to the deceased's pubis. He used a Y instead of a straight line in case the funeral home wanted to put him in an open-collar shirt. When he folded back the ribs with crackling sounds, he commented, "Look here! This man wasn't a smoker; the lungs are healthy-pink."

To illustrate the difference for us students, he ran over to a bank of refrigerators and grabbed a specimen wrapped in plastic sandwich wrap. It was illegal for him to retain any body parts, but, hey, sometimes what you find is so obtuse, you need to bend the rules a bit for the sake of any students who might be smokers. He had us pass the lung tissue sample around. What I saw when it came to me was Saran wrap over a wallet-size piece of lung blacker than ink. Unlike a regular piece of a lung, it was so stiff and hard that if I dropped it, it would have bounced instead of going splat. And when I squeezed it between my index finger and thumb it went *snap-crackle-pop* like a Rice Krispies Treat.

The examiner's gloved fingers felt inside the rib cage, along the right lobes of the lungs to the chest wall below the deceased's shoulder. He tugged theatrically until a segment thwapped out like a busted rubber band. "You have learned about the slippery pleural space between the lungs and the chest wall. This right here is pleurisy. Always painful, but I expect that this man just learned to live with it." Then the doctor cut out the lungs on both sides and plopped them into what I'd call a janitor's bucket positioned on the table next to the deceased's right hip.

Next, stomach, small intestine, large intestine, colon—all okay. The liver, however, was too big, and it looked like it embodied the cirrhosis caused by many-years-long alcohol abuse or hepatitis C. It probably contributed to a paunch when he stood up, the examiner surmised. "He was probably an alcoholic, but the liver was not his immediate cause of death. We need to look farther." It was time for the heart. He sliced it as fine as when you order thick-cut salami at the deli. "Nothing wrong here, either."

Even though I had seen the rainbow colors of cows' intestines at slaughter on my uncle's farm in the Ball Hills in the Mount Rainier forelands, I was still surprised at the reflective hues of the organs inside the peritoneum. Was it all color-coded so that first-year medical students would have an easier time on anatomy exams? The doctor lifted and pulled on the upper and lower intestines, then he sliced the top off the little football-shaped bladder, and he used a sponge to sop out the pee so that we could peer in to see the pointy end where it exited to the urethra and down through the prostate. "Things as expected here, too." A whole bunch more organs were sloshed into the bucket.

Now there was a full external examination of his skin and genitals. Other than the obvious open fracture of the left shoulder, the examiner found nothing that concerned him. I needed to step back so that the doctor could come around to my side of the table to examine the shoulder wound and fracture more closely. The esters and other interior odors and stinks competed with the smell of his fat, which appeared disgustingly similar to the yellow globules on the Albertsons chicken fryer in my fridge back home.

After all these appetizers, it was now time for the main course, the balding, gray-haired head. The examiner noted that the man had shaved recently and that his hair was neatly trimmed. This probably meant that he had a job where he met the public. When the doctor pulled away the wooden block that had been supporting the skull, it clanked onto the stainless-steel table. Both eyelids popped open. I winced. Ow! That must have hurt.

The examiner took a sturdier scalpel to incise all the way around the man's head, being careful not to come down onto the forehead—once again, in consideration of the body's appearance at the funeral. He rolled the skin down over his ears and the back of the neck. Then he took an electric circular saw and buzzed a line around above the ears so that he could pop off a skull cap, which then rolled around noisily on the steel table.

After that, he reached one hand in behind the eyes and lifted the brain out high enough to use pruning shears to clip it at the medulla so it could be pulled away from its connection to the spine. He then placed this human CPU on an eye-level examination platform. Slice after slice, he made his way through the lobes. "Look, fellows. Here is where he had a stroke, but it was not the cause of death that I am looking for. He probably had a heck of a headache for a few months. Now if that stroke had been just five centimeters over this way"—he pointed with his gloved index finger—"he probably would have suffered one-sided paralysis and loss of speech."

"Now, we're onto something, look! This is a cerebral hematoma. It is trauma that is survivable if one gets medical care soon enough. This is why you guys turn on sirens and flashing lights so that a head-injury can go into emergency surgery." The doctor transitioned into his tentative conclusions. This fellow could have banged his head on a concrete floor like the one we're standing on, but the open humerus fracture complicates the story to make such a simple indoor fall unlikely. After he finished, he tossed the brain into the bucket, too.

"The EMT report said that the man, found in his blood-soaked bed, was already stiff, so it looks like his death might not have been reported until, for example, he failed to show up at work for the evening and didn't answer the phone. If he tumbled down a flight of stairs, that could explain his left shoulder. And if he were inebriated, he might have just made his way home and crawled into bed, even though that scenario seems unlikely. Those are just possibilities or theories now. I will ask the police to check the stairways and surrounding area for indicators, such as dribbled blood or maybe even a broken handrail. Even though he's been dead for a while, the toxicology report will tell us if he was drunk at the time of death."

He asked us, "Can you theorize what he did for a living?" Silence, so he began, "His hands are clean, no dirt under his fingernails. No calluses, so he wasn't a manual laborer. A recent haircut. An alcoholic has it easy if he can sneak booze on the job. No wedding ring or evidence of a ring-depression on that finger. My first guess is that he was a divorced bartender."

And then it was over. The medical examiner commended us for our attentiveness and made us laugh nervously when he said that in other classes students had passed out; one guy had even pissed his pants. Then in a final gesture of the macabre, which I suspect he did because he had an audience, he took that big janitor's bucket and poured the contents from about twelve inches above the corpse—plop-ploop-plop—into the open chest and peritoneal cavities. His lips wrinkled into a grin, he said, "It doesn't matter where they go, his body parts just have to all end up inside him when he leaves here."

He stuffed cotton batting into the empty cranium and fitted the skull-cap back in place. After tugging the scalp down and the neck and facial skin up, he sewed it loosely together with big black thread like in an upholstery shop. The cotton was intended to prevent leakage onto the pillow, something that horrifies the bereaved, he stated.

The examiner sewed up the chest and abdomen, too, and pulled the eyelids down over the now drying eyeballs, using drops of super-glue to keep them from popping open again. We students exited into the afternoon sunshine saying hardly a word to one another. The view from the morgue's parking lot was of Seattle's Space Needle, which seemed to be in a different realm from where we students had just been.

That Friday evening after the teaching autopsy, I was to meet Dad and Mom to be their guest for some type of awards banquet in a ritzy downtown Seattle hotel. I had gladly accepted their invitation because it was a chance to see my parents and to eat good food that I didn't have to cook—especially not that fatty yellow chicken fryer in the refrigerator back at my apartment. Dad said it was formal, but that my dark suit would be an adequate substitute for a tuxedo.

A concierge led me to my seat next to my parents at a round table for eight, each place setting defined by crystal stemware and sterling silver cutlery. Soon, another concierge came up and seated a woman and her husband to my right. She exclaimed, "Kristian, it's been a long time, hasn't it?" I nodded and smiled, but I had no idea how long it had been because I had no clue who she was. How would I make it through the next four hours?

She chose the prime rib, which was blood-rare. After she put the first forkful into her mouth, she swallowed, then paused, "You studied in Germany, right? What have you been up to lately? Tell me what you did today." She asked, I answered. Several minutes into my enthusiastic narrative, perhaps after I told her how pink the corpse's lungs were or about the color of the spleen, she set her fork down. A few drops of perspiration dotted her forehead, she burped softly and blotted her lips with the linen napkin. Then she slid her plate up past her dessert spoon toward the floral centerpiece. Finally, she sipped some ice-water out of a crystal goblet and intoned, "Remind me to never, ever ask you what you did today."

6

More Blood

After the first two quarters, the Highline College EMT training program moved into the practicals, held in several local emergency rooms and trauma centers. I was fortunate to be assigned to one of the busiest in the region, Valley Medical Center in Renton. Overnight shifts on Fridays and Saturdays were the most instructive because south King County had lots of drunk drivers. My practice was to sign in on Friday nights at about 11 PM and work up to the end of the "bar rush," when the last victims had been either treated and released, or sent to surgery and admitted to either a hospital room or the Intensive Care Unit, the ICU. I was usually ready to head home around 8 AM.

The emergency department staff was happy to have the extra help, and I was equally happy to be there. I wiped down gurneys (disposing of mud, blood, and urine), recorded blood pressures, assisted with X-rays, and sometimes accompanied the critically injured to the ICU to help the nurses. I still clearly remember a patient with open femur and pelvis fractures that couldn't yet be closed up. The nurses and I winced in sympathy for this young man when he screamed. He had to be lifted in order to change the bedding where he had defecated on himself. Our concern for potential bacterial infection overrode our desire for his comfort.

Back in the ED, the most rewarding task was to watch conscious patients waiting for emergency surgery; sometimes it took an hour or more to assemble the on-call operating room nurses, the anesthesiologist, and the appropriate surgeon or surgeons. I monitored their vital signs and chatted with them, looking intently for the first sign they might lapse into shock.

One time, I was tasked with looking after a 97-year-old man. I went into the next room to report to a surgical resident that his blood pressure seemed to be okay, but that his heart was palpitating wildly. The doctor smiled. "He's 97, was just in an accident, and he's here in the middle of the night; we'd expect that. Keep up your good work."

In Washington State, the "last call" in a bar was supposed to come a half hour before the 2 AM mandatory closing, but some servers pushed the line because no more drinking meant no more tipping. Accordingly, the actual last round of drinks could end up being as late as 1:55 AM. By the time a young man—why was it always a guy?—tossed down "a last one for the road," then stumbled out the door and fumbled with his keys to get into his car, it could be 2:15 AM.

Assuming it takes 20 minutes for the blood alcohol level to peak, after he slipped his keys into the ignition on the fifth try and the engine roared to life, he had become a peril to everyone on the road, including himself. He might charge through a 35 MPH zone at 80, or enter a freeway via its exit ramp only to be befuddled by the array of headlights coming at him.

I routinely drove to Highline College via Des Moines Memorial Drive, so I remember one 24-year-old, my age, who closed out a bar, got into his two-seater Mercedes sports coupe, then thrust the accelerator to the floor using his soon to be fractured right foot. He razzed north through red lights and then wrapped himself and his celebrated piece of automobile-engineering around one of the 1,100 elm trees planted along this boulevard in 1921. They were placed there in memory of the dead from World War I. After this night, I would often think of this young man, too, when I drove this memorial route.

He was transported to Valley Medical Center, where I was on duty that night. In the emergency department there are two entries into the daily log that nobody likes, "D-O-A" (dead on arrival) and "D-I-E" (died in emergency). Although the EMT's kept him hanging on to life, this young man arrived unconscious; he became a D-I-E with us three hours later.

On Fridays, after I signed in and put my sack lunch in the break room, I washed up and put on scrubs. Chores were waiting for me, but if the emergency department remained quiet for a while, I would often find myself chatting with a few nurses and interns over coffee, and maybe some cookies that a nurse brought in. But right around 2 AM, the radio traffic monitors run by the various fire departments would begin to chatter. Tones signaled when a fire department aid car was inbound and from which jurisdiction it was coming. Radio messages also prepared us for the number of victims and severity of injuries. Even so, we held our breath about the carnage we'd see when the ED doors swung open.

One night, I recall being assigned to watch an alert woman in her early sixties who'd been in a head-on with a drunk driver who crossed over the center-line on the Echo Lake Cutoff. This route was a high-speed highway just two lanes wide at the time, connecting I-5 and I-90. While chatting with her, I learned that she was the mother of a fraternity brother of my own younger brother at Washington State University. She and her husband had decided to get an insanely early start from their home in Tacoma for a cross-state drive to Washington State University (WSU) in Pullman. It was parents' weekend.

The woman was brought in with numerous contusions and lacerations, the most severe of which were to her face. She apparently was not seat-belted in, and her head had gone through the windshield, likely leaving pieces of her face dangling from shards of glass. She was astonishingly talkative, despite the vertical gash that splayed her face open from her nostrils to below her mouth, revealing upper and lower teeth and her chin bone. Her husband, the driver, had not arrived in our trauma center with her. She never asked about him, which made things easier for me. I didn't know if he had been flown to Harborview, or if his body was perhaps on the way to the medical examiner.

The wife didn't complain of pain, but said that her face was cold, and she asked if there were pieces of glass on her tongue; it felt so strange. From where I was standing, I could see that there was no glass on her tongue. Then she asked me if I would bring her a hand mirror so she could check for herself. I fibbed, "I'm sorry, we don't have a hand mirror." I feared that if she saw that she looked like a Hollywood movie monster, she'd slip into shock. By now, the operating team was almost ready for her. When she was wheeled away, I told her how much I enjoyed talking with her. I didn't say this, but I hoped that both she and her husband would make it to WSU parents' weekend next year. Maybe they would consider flying.

The sun was up when a 17-year-old appeared under the neon EMERGENCY sign, dropped off by a private car. Other than some makeshift bandages made from a couple of T-shirts around his left hand, he looked fine. When we removed them, we saw a gash across the back of his hand exposing all the tendons to his fingers except for one—the tendon for his middle finger was gone, well not actually gone, but severed with one end pulled toward the finger and the other up into the wrist.

This young man was returning home from his girlfriend's place when he fell asleep at the wheel. He awoke with his car rolling over several times on its way to the bottom of a blackberry-brush ravine. The seat belt held tight while he tumbled, so when he came to rest upside down, he was okay. Releasing the buckle, he fell to the ceiling. The door wouldn't open, and the electric window was dead. Contemplating his situation and after waiting some time, he panicked. Nobody knew where he was, and his car wouldn't be visible from the road above. He bashed out the driver's-side window with his left fist, causing a torrent of blood. He squeezed through the opening and climbed through the brambles up to the road where he waved down a Good Samaritan. That fellow drove him directly to our unit, and I was assigned to help the emergency physician.

The surgical resident that night knew I was an EMT trainee, so he explained what he was doing step by step. "Under other circumstances, we would just need to clean away the damaged tissue and suture the wound inside and at the surface, but the reason that the tendon wasn't visible was that its ends had withdrawn—we don't yet know how far up and away from the wound. He would need emergency surgery to first locate the ends, make sure that they were viable, tug them back together, and then sew them so that they could heal. Delaying the surgery would mean the tendon would continue to contract and that his middle finger would hang useless for the rest of his life. That situation would call for its removal at some date in the future so that the other fingers could function normally." The doctor who was telling me all this was the one who'd be performing the surgery.

I was told to continue to watch this young man, to monitor his blood pressure and—because he had eaten that night—to make sure he didn't vomit and aspirate any regurgitant. One operating room was being cleaned and prepped after the previous, bloody patient, and the staff was calling for another team of operating room nurses and a fresh anesthesiologist. In a moment reminiscent of asking the secretary at Highline if I could be admitted to the EMT program, I asked the surgeon if he would allow me to come into the operating room and watch. He said yes and that he'd alert the head operating room nurse, who would show me how to wash up and get fresh scrubs and a mask for the OR. She was not the least bit pleased, but she had no choice but to do as the surgeon told her. She explained that once we were inside, she would point out where I should stand, and under no circumstances was I to move from there unless she said so.

Now inside the operating room, the surgeon carefully scrutinized the other parts of the young man's body to make sure there would be no surprises. Under normal circumstances, a patient doesn't undergo surgery unless they have been fasting — there is more risk with a full stomach. A nurse inserted a Foley catheter, and the surgeon put a gloved index finger into the youngster's anus. He said it was full, so a nurse placed a "receiving board" that looked rather like a pizza paddle under him in case the anesthesia caused his bowels to release.

The anesthesiologist arrived, obviously sleepy after being roused in the middle of the night. An anesthesiologist's job could be one of hours of monotony punctuated by minutes of terror, and I noticed him nod off once or twice and then shake his head as he woke again. After an hour of cutting and tugging and sewing, the surgeon announced that he had secured both ends of the tendon and that they looked good to go. He said that sutures should perform nicely in helping his young, healthy body create an enduring union of the severed tendon. After several rounds of sewing muscle tissue and skin together, the surgeon was ready to turn this fellow over to the OR nurses for bandages and a splint.

This fortunate young man could probably be released to go home after the anesthesia wore off. There would be follow-up visits and physical therapy in the future. I expected that this kid's parents were probably waiting outside for a post-operation meeting with the surgeon, who would deliver the good news. For my part, I felt privileged to have seen the whole process from him entering the door of the emergency department to him being wheeled out of the OR into the recovery area, the system at its best, bringing a happy ending.

It was now July, and my Friday-Saturday overnight shifts were taking on a familiar rhythm. A biker involved in a serious accident was brought in by EMT aid vehicle to this Renton trauma center. I found the late hour of the morning to be an odd one for the victim of an alcohol-related accident—a fellow sporting a mud-and-blood-caked ponytail—to arrive. I learned it had taken some time to find and extricate him from a ditch on the Auburn-Enumclaw Highway where he and his motorcycle had ended up after the crash. The form said he was 28, but he looked 50. He had a week's worth of stubble, Budweiser breath, and Lucky Strike lines around his eyes. The most frightening thing for me was the fact that his nose had gotten punched up into his skull, and a clear liquid, perhaps cerebrospinal fluid, was fast-dripping out of the wound. A neurosurgeon might find that the meninges, the membranes that protect the brain, had been breached, but that would come during emergency surgery later.

He had so many injuries from head to toe that one long-time emergency department staff member commented that she had rarely seen a patient with as many emergency-medicine modalities all needing to be addressed simultaneously. The EMTs had bandaged him well, but the gauze bandages were thoroughly soaked through, and even when more were added, they continued to drip blood.

Somehow, the man was talkative, well, not talking actually, cursing. The physicians first priority was getting a series of X-rays: inclined, sides, and standing up. He was 6 foot 3, just like me, so I was tasked with assisting the petite X-ray technician on duty. My job was to maneuver this tall man onto a rotating and elevating X-ray table. This was tougher than anything I had been asked to do at Valley Medical Center up until that point. The man wiggled and then thrashed violently, all while yelling profanities. It sure took a new level of determination to stay focused when the patient was yelling things such as, "Get your god-damn hands off me, you fuckin' faggot!"

The guy had barely finished with one "god-fuckin-dammit!" before tossing in another "screw you, you asshole!" We finished in X-ray, and I pushed him— still releasing a stream of invectives—toward the waiting emergency surgery team. After that, the night supervisor told me I could take my break. It was long past my lunch time. The man's blood was smeared on my once clean, light-blue scrubs and on both hands up to my wrists and past my elbows. In those days, AIDS hadn't reared its head across the country, so as a rule folks doing my job didn't need to wear gloves unless we had a cut on our hands or unless there was obvious pus on the patient. We just washed up again and again with antibacterial soap.

I headed for the break room and grabbed my paper sack from the fridge containing a baloney sandwich, Twinkies, and an apple. The coffee maker had been turned off hours earlier, but I was able to eke out one more cold cup. At the break room sink, I washed my forearms and scrubbed my hands. I had just wolfed down the first half of the sandwich when I flashed back to that inaugural evening class at Highline College when the firefighters had tossed around the gruesome details of a fiery head-on collision. I wondered then if I was cut out to handle this stuff. Then I noticed some of the biker's dried blood still on the back of my hands. I stepped over to the sink to wash up once more. As blood-pink soap suds went down the drain, I said to myself, "I think I've answered that question pretty well."

Artist Point

I brought my ice axe along and wore gaiters atop my boots for a solo hike on early-summer snow to Artist Point above the Mount Baker Ski Area in Washington State. A sunglasses-wearing, under-equipped woman appeared in the distance; she was clearly having problems maintaining her balance in the softening snow, but there was no danger because the slope where she walked was gentle. I made my way over to her, and she began to ply me with questions. She gazed at magnificent Mt. Baker and asked, "Do people climb that mountain?" I responded, "Yes." Then she asked if they needed to have special equipment, "Do they need to wear croutons?"

I instantly imagined crampon spikes stabbing pieces of crisped bread on a giant green salad. I turned toward Mt. Shuksan so she couldn't see my grin and answered her, "Yes, they need special equipment."

7

Svelte

In 1974, Kathy was a flight attendant, back when they were still called stewardesses. Chic in her tailored uniform and high heels, she cared for first-class passengers traveling between North America and Asia. Friends from our church thought that I should start acting more like an eligible bachelor. In other words, take a pause from hiking and skiing and ask Kathy out.

The most important indoor event on my fall calendar was the *Mountaineers* annual banquet, so I decided to invite Kathy. It was held in the largest ballroom at a hotel in Bellevue, an affluent city on the east shore of Lake Washington, and it put some of my friends in a quandary. They didn't own a suit and tie. Few of the climbers I knew even owned a sports jacket, but if they did, this would be the night to wear it. Most, however, just came in heavy wool slacks and their best Pendleton wool shirt. My date, Kathy, said yes to my invitation.

I had explained to Kathy that this year's banquet speaker would be Pete Schoening*, who had recently returned from leading the American Expedition to the Russian Pamirs during an international convocation of several national expeditions organized in conjunction with an agency in the Soviet Government. (The Pamirs are the orographic crux of all the highest mountain ranges of Central Asia: the Himalaya, the Karakoram, the Tian Shun, the Altay, and the Urals.)

In my teenage Basic Climbing Course years, Pete Schoening had surmounted the hero-pedestal in my personal pantheon. For me as a kid, he was not just a legend for his first ascents and colossal deeds, but because he paid attention to me, a 14-year-old boy taking the *Mountaineers* course and just beginning to learn the ropes—figuratively and literally.

Around the world, Pete Schoening is known for his ascents of Everest, Gasherbrum One, and Mount Vinson in Antarctica. But by far, his most fêted accomplishment was when in 1953 he executed the "miracle belay." On the Abruzzi Ridge of K2, all by himself, Schoening arrested the fall of six climbers, who would have otherwise plunged to their deaths. Pete's standing hip belay on K2 was roughly similar to, but far more consequential than the sitting hip belay that my buddy Peter was executing on Mount Erie before the rock clobbered him between the eyes. [*Chapter 4*]

An honor for me, but of zero significance to Kathy, we happened to be seated at a table with Dee Molenaar, author and biographer. Dee was one of those six men Pete Schoening had saved on K2. Kathy, svelte and stunning, attempted small talk with the other couples at our table. However, when it came to Dee in his red wool shirt and bolo tie, she demurred.

Schoening's after-dinner program was a narrated slide presentation starting with flying into the Pamirs from Moscow in a combination commercial-military Aeroflot jet in the old Soviet Union. The team then traveled over primitive roads in military transports, going ever higher until, at last, the American team that he led forsook the trucks and charged up the slopes of rock and ice in their high-altitude mountaineering gear. Hurricane-force winds at sub-zero temperatures buffeted them. Collapsing snow-bridges. Falling seracs. Below-zero temperatures. Even an earthquake. But amazingly even though there were fatalities in the other nations' teams during the same period, Pete had managed to bring every American back home safely, with many of them successfully summiting. The eyes of everyone in the room—except Kathy's—were riveted by Pete's narration and the giant glowing slide screen.

At the conclusion of the presentation, Schoening announced that he would distribute the *Mountaineers* Climbing Division's awards for that year. After a few others, he called my name to come up to receive my *Six Peak Pin*, awarded for ascending the "six majors" in Washington State. I was humbled because as I walked up to the podium, Pete told everyone that this pin represented a huge accomplishment. But how could this giant among alpinists say that? Similarly, the President of Harvard wouldn't congratulate a high school boy for getting into honors English. Even so, I brimmed with pride when he handed me the little jewelry box and shook my hand. Back at the table, Kathy examined the pin's tiny gold peaks on a blue enamel horizon, and said, "That's so cute."

When the lights came up and it was time to go, I helped Kathy in her high heels to step back up into my backroads-ready Ford Bronco. The half-hour drive to her place near Sea-Tac Airport was nearly silent. At the front door of her English-style cottage, a jet roared overhead. When it was quiet again, I told her I hoped she enjoyed the evening. She thanked me and summed everything up with these words, the last ones we ever exchanged, "It looked cold."

---

*   A month after the banquet, a mutual friend clued me in that Kathy thought that I was inviting her to dinner and a "peach showing," not to a mountaineering presentation by Pete Schoening.

Self-portrait of young me, gazing at Gothic Peak, in Monte Cristo area of Washington State's Cascades.

8

Facing Destruction

The events that befell the *RMS Titanic* on the fateful date of April 14, 1912, are portrayed in the 1958 film *A Night to Remember*, based on survivor accounts. According to these fortunate ones, the ship's officers were calm while a string ensemble played *Nearer My God to Thee*, a hymn written seven decades before their collision with the iceberg. Some panic did break out in several areas, mostly regarding getting into the limited number of lifeboats. It might just be screenplay, but an infamous few were said to have used trickery such as dressing in women's clothing in order to get into the "women and children first" lifeboats. After the lifeboats were all launched, most on the upper decks were at peace, despite the fact that in less than an hour they would drown in the North Atlantic.

How can a person be calm when facing destruction? When I did my EMT training at the trauma center, I saw people with a resolve similar to those Titanic victims. There was peaceful resolution among people who understood that everything they knew about life had just changed. They might not live to see another morning, yet they remained calm. As I wrote in Chapter 6, there were other humans in the ED—often intoxicated—who became venomous cobras flaring their hoods and hissing, even though they, too, would be toe-tagged in the morgue if not that night, then the next. How does one satisfactorily explain these behavioral differences?

The following hypothetical illustration of crisis attempts to speak to the question above. The catastrophic wrist injury in this narrative is, however, real. In 1965 as a PE football lineman in freshman activities at PLU, I was outclassed by my opponent, who the season before had been a State of Idaho Allstar. When I found myself airborne, flying backwards, I stupidly stuck out my left hand to stop me. As in the story below, the injury was catastrophic. We don't know what happened to the guy in the story you are about to read, but in my case, the recovery was long but miraculous.

> *You bump your head on the kitchen cabinet door that junior left open for the 20th time. You slam it hard, and it falls off its hinges and hits your slippered foot. Junior is sleeping overnight at a friend's house, so you can't yell at him. Nevertheless, you are agitated and scream in pain.*
>
> *You end up late to meet your buddy for tennis because you had to put Band-Aids and Neosporin on your foot, while also reinstalling the kitchen cabinet door. When at last you're on the tennis court, you are not on your game. You blame your son for this.*
>
> *You trip while attempting an easy backhand return. You should know better, but instead of rolling, you stick out your left arm to catch your fall. But when your hand hits the clay, it sticks tight. Searing pain hits your brain, and you turn to look. Your radius and ulna have broken off in your wrist, which is now a scattering of joint fragments, and, while the skin is still attached, the hand hangs useless below all these pieces of bone.*
>
> *Are you mad at your son now? Do you care that your tennis buddy just watched you be a total klutz? No, in one second, your life has just been turned upside down. Your tennis friend, nauseous at the sight, runs to his jacket and grabs his cellphone to*

call 9-1-1. In the eight minutes it takes the EMTs to arrive, you observe calmly that the useless hand has started to balloon around your fingers from the internal hemorrhage. The EMTs ask you how you are doing. You wince out, "I've had better days."

If all goes well, modern orthopedic surgery will put you back together in a few weeks, and after months of physical therapy, you might once again be able to use that hand to hug your son.

Here is another hypothetical example of true grist. The synthesized elements of this story are drawn from accounts that I heard from various *Mountaineers* friends at different times and on different peaks. This is an example of a situation where the person who has endured the accident is not the only one able to enter "crisis-management mode." Friends and bystanders can also become empowered as on-the-spot superheroes.

An open femur fracture after a high angle rock-climbing fall. A shout, "Bruce, take off your T-shirt and try to shove it right here under the palm of my hand where I'm applying pressure. Jan, would you grab my first aid kit out of the topmost section of my pack? There are two sterile-wrapped hemostats at the bottom of the left pocket. Could you please bring them to me? Susan, I know you are a runner, could you first geo-locate us on the topo and then take another runner with you to go out to where there's cellphone reception and call Mountain Rescue? The rest of you need to scout out a helicopter landing place and figure out a good way to get Sheldon to it once we have stabilized him here.

A week later, Sheldon is out of intensive care and in a regular hospital room. After progressive visitations, the 11 other climbers reunite at a Starbucks to celebrate the camaraderie they had achieved in making it possible for Sheldon to live. The guy who dropped into the role of emergency response leader was not the climb leader; that was Sheldon himself. The one who became the de facto rescue leader, was the belayer below when Sheldon's human protection devices pulled out one after the other. Over lattés they concurred that they were united as a team now, and they would want to continue in their camaraderie into the future, and not just on climbs.

Back to a real-life story. This is a first-person account of a hike gone wrong. Longtime friend Frank, age 58, and his son Lew, age 10, and I, age 45, embarked on a spring trip involving some steep snow and easy ridge running. In Kittitas County on the east side of the Cascades, we drove to the Ingalls Pass trailhead at the end of the Teanaway River Road. It was May, so we expected to find the trail buried in snow soon after leaving the car. We all had ice axes. Lew had a kid-size MSR model.

The plan was to ascend toward Longs Pass so that Frank could show me in the distance where a few years before he had fallen on the exposed West Ridge of Mount Stuart. Frank's belayer saved his life that day. After the party tended to Frank's scrapes, they summited and set up their planned overnight bivouac. As planned, they exited the mountain the next morning via Ulrich's Couloir.

After Frank's narration of his Stuart fall, the three of us hiked over toward the foot of Ingalls Peak, where we ate a late lunch. Lew didn't weigh much, so he walked on top of the snow's breakable crust, while Frank and I post-holed deep into it, making for laborious forward progress. Accordingly, we tried to stay on snow-free ridges and rock outcroppings as much as possible.

Later that afternoon, we took another break to admire the granite slabs of the three summits of Ingalls Peak. Now, we saw that the way back down to the trail and eventually to the car would be a slog in soft snow. That was unless we took a shortcut via the descent of two cliffs, a bit steep, but with bucket-like handholds and footholds. Frank assured me that Lew, a wiry natural at climbing, would have no problem. Even so, he took Lew's ice axe in the same hand as his own so that Lew could have both of his free.

I strapped my own ice axe onto my pack so that I had two unencumbered hands. We negotiated the first face with ease. But the second pitch, roughly the height of a four-story building with a steep snow run-out at the bottom, was more mountain than either Frank or I had expected on our "hike." Even so, we continued to down-climb, rather than backtracking as we should have. I tended right, while Frank got Lew started down a gully to the left. Frank was facing out like I was, and he was about 25 feet above me and to my left. I heard a thud, and instantly I knew what the noise meant. Frank's airborne body sailed past me. He bounced hard two more times before the cliff spit him onto the snow. Frank lay motionless as his body slid another 30 feet down the snowfield. As I hurried down, I called Frank's name, but he didn't respond. When I arrived at his side, he was conscious and breathing, but quiet, so I started a quick assessment. He was bleeding from both hands and had gashes on his forehead and nose, as well as some others on his scalp. Neither Frank's nor Lew's ice axe was anywhere to be seen.

Lew had completed his down-climb and was now standing 10 feet above me, shaking but silent. I pulled my puffy, insulated parka out of my pack and held Lew's hand as I brought him to a small ledge. Lew was so little and my parka so big that he disappeared inside it. In a couple minutes he fell asleep and rested there until it was time for us to leave. What was it that enabled this boy to sleep when nearby his father was facing a life-threatening crisis?

The contents of my first-aid kit were spread about us on the snow. To my relief, Frank was talking and the pupils of his eyes responded normally. He lifted his head off my pillow of extra clothes to see that Lew was okay, too. I used Band-Aids on his smaller cuts, but on his right hand and especially on his forehead and scalp, I used nearly all of my tape and gauze. Frank now sported a white blood-stained beanie that made him look like he was coming off being treated by a medic on Omaha Beach. I still wondered where the two errant ice axes had gone. Frank also had a gash across his nose that would need sutures, but it had stopped bleeding, so I decided to leave it because a large bandage would obscure his vision.

Frank complained that it hurt when he tried to move his left leg. My mistake! I hadn't considered his legs, which were inside heavy wool trousers. When I looked behind his left knee, I cringed. No need to look any further for Frank's ice axe, as it was buried in the snow beneath his knee, pick down and adze up. That top-rear blade, the adze, had cut through the fabric and penetrated all the way to the shaft behind the knee. I was surprised and relieved that there was comparatively little blood in his pant leg or on the snow.

I said nothing to him about what I saw. I assumed but didn't know that the adze, which is a bit larger than two inches wide and three inches long, had penetrated into the space between the ligaments and tendons

100

behind the knee itself. I decided to prepare for a risky course of action because I thought it best to see if Frank could walk out, rather than stay put and try for a mountain rescue. A helicopter might not arrive until the next day, and we would have to survive a below-freezing night. Frank needed emergency medical care, and I feared at any moment he might lapse into shock.

So, while I was prepared for the worst with an array of pressure bandages, I asked, "Frank, can you get up?" I hoped that the adze of his ice axe would drop out the way it entered without tearing anything else. Wonderful! The axe pulled out and landed on the snow as I hoped it would. I still didn't tell Frank about where it had been; he'd need to use it as a walking stick to limp his way back to the car. I simply told him that he had a cut there, which I needed to bandage before we started our hike back to the trailhead. Obviously, I didn't let on that I wondered if he'd be able to walk at all. I figured that in the next few minutes we'd both find out. Frank favored that left leg, but he ambulated better than I expected. On the trail we met a party of four. One woman looked at his face and head bandages and gasped, "Good God! What happened to you?" And she hadn't even seen the hole behind his knee.

Only when we were back in the car and headed for the emergency room in Cle Elum did I tell Frank about where I discovered his ice axe. In Cle Elum, the emergency department doctor removed and refreshed my bandaging and installed two surgical drains behind his left knee. He didn't stitch up his forehead or nose, though, because he wanted Frank to see a surgeon in Seattle that specializes in facial surgery to handle that delicate operation.

Even after my move to Alaska, Frank and I remained the best of friends for years. Lest I forget, I discovered Lew's ice axe buried even deeper under Frank's in the snow that day. Lew grew taller, and he outgrew the small ice axe, so Frank gave it to me for my son Evan. It flew in my luggage back to Anchorage after a trip to Seattle, and it hung on a hook next to my own in my garage on Snowflake Drive. Finally, Evan was too tall for it, as well, so I gave it to another kid in Anchorage.

9

Yes, That's a Body

California's idealists had John Muir; Washington State's idealists had Paul Wiseman. Paul graduated from Portland, Oregon's Reed College in 1933. Sinewy, tall, and rarely frowning, Paul was twice president of the *Mountaineers*. He was indefatigable in striving to preserve mountain wildernesses, and he also took time to mentor youngsters such as me. I cannot think of anybody who didn't like Paul, except perhaps for the board members of Port Angeles and Tacoma paper mills. Lady-friend climbers through the years told me of being smitten with Paul. Alas for them, Paul never married. His roommate at Reed College, Hunter, remained his lifelong companion. Paul and Hunter led separate lives, but they always returned to their domicile in Olympia, Washington.

In 1928, Paul Wiseman was a 16-year-old Boy Scout on an expedition to explore the southern peaks of Washington's Olympic Peninsula. In the following years, he became a tireless advocate working to motivate the U.S. Congress to create Olympic National Park, which they did in 1938.

On the 1928 Boy Scout trip, Paul made the first ascents of the 6,378-foot White Mountain and its neighbor, 6,417-foot Mount La Crosse. Fifty years later in September 1978, he led a group of five *Mountaineers* to celebrate the golden anniversary of those two first-ascents. I was beyond pleased to be on that anniversary climb roster.

We used to call it Indian Summer, but whatever the nomenclature, the weather on the Olympic Peninsula during the climb was a reinvention of warm summer days, but with deeply shadowed, moss-dripping, cool valleys. The summits had no hint of white yet, and they basked in sunshine beneath an azure sky. We hiked to base camp along the Dosewallips River Trail and dropped our overnight gear at Camp Siberia. There I got the bejeezuz scared out of me when I noticed a sow black bear 10 feet to my left and her two cubs five feet to my right. To my relief, she just huffed at her kids, and they all ambled off into the brush. While setting up my tent, my heart rate dropped to normal again. Given that our group planned on possibly not returning to camp before dark, we prepared our site sooner, rather than later under the dim light of our headlamps.

Our first destination was the summit of White Mountain. Even though Paul rarely paid attention to Fred Becky's *Climbers Guide to the Cascades and Olympics*, he led us up the standard route listed in the book. It was, after all, the route that he, himself, had established as a kid. Soon, the forest gave way to sub-alpine firs, the vistas growing in light and in tinges of fall color with every upward step. As we gained altitude, we looked over a glacier-capped sea of summits to the north, down the Dosewallips Valley at the little hanging glaciers nearby, and across a divide to the summit of Mount La Crosse, the next day's destination.

The summit pyramid of White Mountain was easy, but exposed. In the autumn sunshine and stillness we found at the top, Paul regaled us with Boy Scout stories. All was jolly from our summit vantage until we peered back down to the col, the pass between mountain massifs, that was the route of our ascent. At the spot where we had dropped off our heavier packs and ice axes so that we could climb in shirtsleeves to the top, we noted that five snow-white mountain goats had moved in on our gear. Those perennially salt-starved critters were after our sweat. We couldn't see, but they were no doubt licking our ice axe straps and backpacks and waist bands. What could we do but hope that they didn't get the urge to chew? When we got back to the col, it turned out that there was no irreparable damage, just a few souvenir teeth marks.

Although in 1978 this cross-Olympics trail was already on its way to becoming a hiking classic, we were by ourselves. The crescendo of springtime snowmelt waterfalls was at a rest. Most of the birds had already retreated to the lowlands because they knew that winter was just a couple weeks away. Summer's voluptuous foliage, the *false hellebore* and *cow parsnip*, were rotting. Especially the dead cow parsnip, also known as *bear's bane*, stunk. The occasional whiff of the stench wasn't bad, a bit like the way the cow manure smell in dairy country on the breeze lends a pastoral vibe.

After not too long, we got back to our tents and dinner—that was after retrieving the food that we'd hung between trees beyond the reach of bears. The next morning, as planned, Paul went to each tent to rouse us to meet the dawn's faintest glimmer. The hissing roar of MSR stoves pierced the silence as each of us made our coffee and whatever we'd brought along for breakfast. We zipped up the doors to the tents and we followed Paul on his own uncharted route toward La Crosse. The way up through a series of cliff bands, couloirs, and rock spines would be more "interesting" than the ordinary route, Paul explained, not letting on that he wasn't certain about the way up.

It was cold on the shadowy side of La Crosse, but our brisk climbing warmed our muscles. We took occasional short rests, and after we were about three hours from camp, Paul seemed to be struggling to find the best way toward the top. It wasn't that we were "off route," as we hadn't even been on a known route to begin with. Somehow, the stench of bear's bane decay in the air had gotten stronger, which seemed odd because we had left those rotting plants far below us.

Following one another, we all concentrated on climbing. Because we needed to keep three of our four extremities (hands and feet) in contact with the rock while moving one at a time, something that demands concentration, we weren't looking around. The rock spine we were ascending was just eight feet to the right of a dry couloir, a magnificent gully that would be full of avalanche snow in the spring and summer. I was bringing up the rear of our six-climber line, and because the rock was convex above me, I didn't have a line of sight on any of the others.

It was then that a young woman above me yelled, "Is that a body?" I yelled back to her, "What do you mean? A deer? A marmot?" Her exasperated reply came, "No! A body. You know, a body-body." By this time, the fellow above her had stopped climbing and turned around. He stated with a seeming nod to British humour, "Yes, that is a body."

Now, we all knew the source of the stink was not vegetable in nature. The corpse was aligned with the couloir, head up, feet down. The empty-eyed skull's neck gazed back up toward the summit. A mane of long, black hair was still attached in back. The upper body was an assemblage of bones clad in a black fisherman's-knit sweater. Inexplicably, it was partially cinched up so that some of the rib cage was visible. It was obviously a male, about six-feet-tall. The bones of both arms and all fingers were still attached. There were no rings on any of the fingers. But at the waist, under tan cargo shorts with a mesh belt, the fellow transitioned from a skeleton into gray, bloated legs and bare feet. The skin was stretched so tight it looked like it would explode with a pin prick. Where were his socks and boots?

We were standing very close to him. His mouth was open, and it was clear he had benefited from good dental care. Perhaps the most doleful thing was the way the eye holes in the skull seemed to be focused up and away toward the precipices of La Crosse from where he had evidently fallen.

We all gathered on three small step-like ledges beside the corpse. In stunned silence, we regarded the remains of a man, who months before had been a fellow lover of the mountains. Paul asked, "What would you like to do?" Nobody wanted to climb. We decided to figure out a way to notify a park ranger, if we could find one. Our maps showed a ranger station about three hours' distance by trail to the west. Would it still be staffed in September? Two from our party volunteered to descend to the trail and make a dash for the station. We figured they could be back to Camp Siberia in time to break camp that evening, at which point we could head out together to the Dosewallips trailhead where our cars were parked.

For us four that remained, the trip back to camp started out somber, but gradually the chatter of camaraderie sprang up again. As we down-climbed, we tied yellow plastic tape (we carried wanding tape in our packs) onto bushes to mark the way for the body to be eventually recovered.

We guessed as to why this fellow was evidently climbing alone, and why he was up high on the flanks of Mount La Crosse. Where was his pack? Where were his sunglasses? Did he even have a watch? He certainly must have had an ice axe, too. I submitted that because the upper body was a skeleton, it had been exposed to the air and scavenging birds all summer. After falling from the heights, he probably plunged feet-first into the soft snow of the couloir. By late summer, all the refrigeration of his lower body would have disappeared.

So apparently, it hadn't been very long ago that his legs and feet had decayed into the bloated balloons we witnessed.

Paul admitted that his route-finding skills might not have been as good as he had initially thought. There were Class 5 cliff bands above the area where the body was found, and we weren't prepared for them. We had no ropes and no seat harnesses. Paul likely would have called off the climb, anyway.

Back at Camp Siberia, we made coffee and chatted. The pair returned from the ranger station with daylight to spare. It had turned out that while the ranger was preparing to close up for the season, it had still been occupied. The ranger radio-relayed Olympic National Park Headquarters in Port Angeles, and he was ordered to hike up to the couloir and camp next to the body while awaiting the body's retrieval.

The pair that had raised the alarm were dumb-founded by the order. They shouted into the microphone, "No! No! No! It's a rock face. There's no place for a tent. Even if there were any hikers around now, nobody in their right mind—er, ah, hmm—would go up there!" Headquarters relented and told the ranger to take a partner and hike there the following day, to take photos and draw a diagram for a report, and to be ready to guide a body retrieval party from the coroner's office after the State Patrol determined the appropriate jurisdiction, probably in a couple more days.

We left Camp Siberia and headed down the Dosewallips Trail to our cars. I followed Paul so that we could chat. I queried him about the other climbs that he had recently led. He was in his sixties, so I asked, "Paul, you are climbing in the mountains nearly every weekend. Don't you ever get pains that make you want to quit?" He answered, "Of course, I do. But if I paid attention to the aches, pains, and protests of my poor bones, I'd never do anything."

Then and there, I cemented a decision that I wanted to be like Paul.

Postscripts

A month later, *The Seattle Times* reported that the Washington State Patrol had compared trailhead registries from the southern half of the park with the names in its database of missing persons. There was a match. On the Dosewallips sign-in sheets from late May to early June a male's name matched. He had signed in for a solo trek to the Pacific Ocean side of the park. He turned out to be an Evergreen State College student from the Midwest, and his parents had reported him missing to the Washington State Patrol because he never showed up back home after spring term had ended. The newspaper speculated that he had hitchhiked to the trailhead with plans to hitchhike back out to civilization from a trailhead on the opposite side of the park, explaining why there was no car abandoned at either the eastern or western trailhead.

Reed College's alumni publication, *REED MAGAZINE 2013, multiple entries:*

Distinguished alumnus and philanthropist Paul Wiseman was an active climb-leader with the Mountaineers *into his eighties, and he could be found in the wilderness mountains much of the time after he retired from leading. His climbing boots were hung up for good in 2011, two days before his 99th birthday.*

Anderson Peak and Glacier, near Mount La Crosse and White Mountain.

Part Three

Accident Investigations in Alaska

This section continues where Chapter 1 and Chapter 2 left off. I had secured my dream job as a licensed, resident casualty adjuster in the State of Alaska. Because of my prior experience in emergency medicine and mountaineering, my work assignments soon became the catastrophes involving injury, blood, and death.

Whether you are an auto mechanic who can't work because some dolt rear-ended you at a red light and gave you whiplash, or you are a single mom, perhaps a waitress, who learned that her trailer burned to the ground with her two kids inside; the needs are the same. Respect. Compassion. Help.

The following stories are a sampling of the insurance claims across Alaska that I handled. They are not the worst, not the bloodiest, not the saddest, and—it might be hard to believe—but there are even funnier claims stories than the ones recounted here. The selected stories provide a portrait of me working in the best job I could have hoped for, and in the place I love more than any other, Alaska.

Thrush singing from a snag in a clear-cut on Prince of Wales Island.

10

Blue Dress with Long Sleeves

Nome is on the south side of the Seward Peninsula, which thrusts west toward Siberia. This town is the finish line of the Iditarod Trail Dog Sled Race, which runs 1,049 miles from Anchorage to Nome. Tourists sometime confuse the name "Seward Peninsula" with the "Kenai Peninsula," where the cruise-ship port of Seward is located—on Resurrection Bay, adjacent to Kenai Fjords National Park. The peninsula where Nome lies is far to the north and west, and it is bisected by the Arctic Circle.

117

Nome could define the word "improbable." It has no natural harbor, no forests, no navigable river; if not for the "other" Gold Rushes of the 1890's, it wouldn't exist. By 1899, gold-seekers and scoundrels had poured in, and judges—empowered by scurrilous connections to Seattle—rendered judgments that enabled the pervasive crimes of claim jumping with the judges on the take from the claim jumpers themselves.

What was the draw for 20,000 miners (including hoodlums and dance hall girls; and even the gunslinger Wyatt Earp of Tombstone fame) to hop barely seaworthy steamers sailing from Seattle or San Francisco to Nome? Well, gold could be picked up by hand on the beaches! Even today, some summer gold-panners are able to make a hard-sought living panning for gold on the shore of Norton Sound lying within walking distance of Nome's Front Street.

By 1910, the Gold Rushes that had made some people rich were mostly over. Wyatt Earp moved to nearby St. Mary's on the Yukon River, where he became sheriff. At close to 4,000 residents today, Nome is still a big city by Alaskan standards.

There are 16 permanently inhabited villages on the 20,600 square miles of the Seward Peninsula. Two of these permanent settlements, Golovin and White Mountain, my personal favorites, are Iditarod checkpoints for dog sled teams in the final segment of the race, the dash west up Norton Sound and under the burled arch in Nome.

Though the name "Olson" doesn't sound typically Inupiaq Eskimo, it is indeed a well-known surname in both Golovin and Nome. The very first Olson was a 19th century explorer from Norway. Olson Air Service had its roots in Golovin, and its storied chief pilot was Emo Olson, who perished in a landing accident. His sister, "Sister" née Margaret, then took over the business and ran it from the Nome airport for a number of years.

Sister told me that Emo wasn't her brother's real name. As a little tyke, he tried to say, "I am Eskimo," but it came out as "I'm Emo," and it stuck. Now, there was just one girl among the Olson boys, the sister, and that is how she came to be called Sister, even though countless people over the years mistook her name for a title, thinking she was a nun. Sister was the one who had supplied me with the muktuk, harvested from the village of Savoonga on Saint Lawrence Island [*Chapter 1*]. Flying into Savoonga across the water to the west, if you are lucky, you can catch a glimpse of the mountains of the Chukchi Peninsula in Russia's Far East before your plane glides down to the gravel runway.

In the summer of 1996, a twenty-something Golovin single mom—I'll call her Bernice—got a summer job at Nome's fish processing plant. She flew in with her two-

and-a-half-year-old daughter, securing a tiny company apartment on the banks of Nome's Snake River Slough. While she was at work in the cannery, other Inupiat Native women working different shifts would share the duties of watching around a half-dozen children. Typical of Western Alaska, there wasn't any grass around, just an expanse of river gravel and rocks that ran down from the worker cabins to the beach. This play area for kids doubled as the road in and out of the apartments.

Nobody living in the cannery apartments had a car. They walked out the back of the apartments to work, and if they needed to go anywhere else, they called a taxi. One windless day, the children were riding their trikes and bikes with training wheels when a jet skier razzing around on the slough grabbed their attention. They all pedaled down to the shoreline to view the spectacle. Accordingly, the kids were now playing in the middle of what might otherwise be considered the driveway. Bernice was at work, and it never became clear who else was supposed to be watching the children at the time.

A taxi came in off the Nome Airport Highway and drove over the gravel to drop off his passenger in front of one of the apartments. Bernice's daughter chose that moment to pedal her tricycle up the gentle incline toward her own doorway. Taxis are often in a hurry, time is money. The taxi van reversed quickly and tragically thumped over the tricycle and the little girl.

Someone ran screaming to the processing plant to get Bernice. She was on the scene even before the Nome Fire Department paramedics. Bernice scooped her daughter into her arms, and she saw that her little chest was caved in and blood oozed in a tire track pattern from wounds in both arms. Bernice tried to hold her struggling daughter and sop up some of the blood with her own sweatshirt. By the time EMTs arrived, her little girl had stopped moving. It was tough for Bernice to hand her over to the paramedics, but she knew they were her last hope.

The paramedics worked to resuscitate the girl for a long time, with Bernice sitting next to them inside the aid car. When they drove to the hospital, Bernice accompanied her daughter. The hospital was not far away—nothing in Nome is. There, the emergency room doctor told Bernice what she already knew. In the kindest words he could muster, he said her little girl had passed on. She was for that emergency department a D-O-A, dead on arrival.

In Anchorage, I got the call from Ron Fly, senior complex claims examiner in Omaha, one of the most ethically courageous men I've ever known. National Indemnity Company, a Berkshire-Hathaway Company, was the taxi's insurer. Before I knew it, I was on the next jet to Nome. Upon landing and picking up my rental car, I drove to my friend June Engstrom's little house on Fourth Avenue, which she ran as a B&B. June, the entrepreneur, often gave up her own bedroom and slept in the garage if she had more than two guests. My job was to assemble all the facts, meet with the witnesses, and see what could be done to lend a helping hand in the tragedy.

The taxi driver, a young man, was in police custody and not yet allowed to talk to anyone—the cops told me he wasn't in the mental state to do so, anyway. That was okay. I would be in Nome for a few days, and I could wait to get his story. In the meantime, I interviewed the investigating officer, and later got a hold of the report made by the Nome Police. On my last morning in town, the driver would ultimately be able to give me his statement.

On my first full day in Nome, I searched for Bernice; I wasn't surprised that she'd vacated her cannery apartment. Sister Olson told me she was probably in a large house with several members of Bernice's extended family. I drove to that address, knocked, and was ushered into the back of the largest room in the house. There were two concentric circles of folding chairs. The women, including Bernice, were seated inside, and the men were in the outer circle. Several men were pounding out a rhythm on traditional, circular, sealskin drums. Most of them were singing Native songs that to my Western ears sounded chant-like. I took a seat just outside the men's circle.

After perhaps half an hour, Bernice, who had not taken part in the songs, stood to her feet and shrieked. Everyone fell silent. She spoke, "My daughter is lying dead in the hospital, and there isn't even anybody to wash the blood off her arms."

In the moments that followed, Bernice explained that her child was still dressed in the clothes she wore at the time of her death. Bernice had no money for a proper funeral and no means to return to Golovin for the burial. Perhaps the most poignant thing Bernice said was that her daughter's face still looked as sweet as ever. Even if her relatives could fly in from the outlying villages, she didn't want them to see the tire tracks of the taxi on her daughter's arms.

I waited until Bernice finished and stood up. When the whole group turned to look at me, I explained that I was there on behalf of the taxi driver's insurance company. "I have no words to express my sorrow, but I can fix the money-related problems. If Bernice wants me to, I will arrange the details for the funeral according to her instructions."

Moments later, I made an emergency phone call to Ron Fly, after hours, at his home in Omaha. He authorized me to do whatever I deemed necessary, and he told me not to worry about the budget. There was plenty of liability insurance available on the policy, but the point now was to help. (A cynic might chide here that this was just the company's effort to "keep the cost of the claim under control." It wasn't. Ron and the people he worked with did good work because they were compassionate human beings.)

I assembled Bernice and five of her closest family members to plot out the next steps. There is no funeral home in Nome, so Bernice's daughter would need to be flown to an Anchorage undertaker for embalming and placement in an appropriate child's casket. Bernice specified that she wanted her in a blue dress, her favorite color, but with long sleeves so that during viewing people wouldn't see the wounds on her arms above her wrists.

It took me two days to get everything arranged. Alaska Airlines would fly her body to Anchorage, where the funeral home would receive it. The hardest part was tracking down a little girl's blue dress with long sleeves. I found it at JC Penney at Anchorage's Fifth Avenue Mall, and the sweet saleslady even said she would personally drive it to the funeral home on her break.

It turned out there would be two funerals, one in the Lutheran church in Nome, and five days later, another traditional Native ceremony at the Golovin cemetery. I arranged for an open charge account at Bering Air for relatives from all over the Seward Peninsula and up into Kotzebue to be flown into Nome, and then east to Golovin. While taking care of the arrangements,

I ran into Bernice's mom. She said to me in broken English a phrase that I'll always cherish, "I can see that you're a real cool guy."

On day four, my work was finally done, and all the complex arrangements had been finalized. So, on a sunny summer evening I took the Alaska Airlines 737-200 Combi (the front half of the aircraft reserved for freight) back to Anchorage. I had the front window seat on the left side of the plane, just in front of the wing. As we climbed out of Nome and started over Norton Sound, the coast came into view under the dazzling Alaska summer nighttime sunshine, and then below me the village of Golovin. In that moment, the weight of what I had been doing struck me. I wiped tears from my eyes.

After the case was closed, I received a courtesy report from Ron Fly. All had gone well with the Nome attorney, and the estate settlement for the little girl was both equitable and generous. The bills for airfare and funeral services were all paid, along with significant compensatory damages to the mom. But I wondered to myself, how do you calculate the value of a dead little girl? I was glad it was him, not me, that had to do it.

11

Bingo!

For a lot of Alaskans, bingo is like church, only better. But bingo parlors are dangerous. Twisted ankles, dislocated shoulders, fractured patellas. And because bingo is most popular in winter, broken ankles and sprained wrists are the risks posed by parking lots, especially if one doesn't plan on wearing ice cleats to get to into the building. Patrons generally pad around on the carpet in Nikes or Adidas or something similar.

The typical commercial insurance policy in Alaska includes no-fault "premises medical payments" (med-pay) coverage, generally with a $10,000 limit.

That means that all one needs to do to get medical bills paid is to have an accident—typically a slip-and-fall—on the insured premises. So, even if you trip over your own shoelaces, your medical expenses will get paid. If the costs exceed the med-pay limit, then there must be provable negligence on the part of the insured for the liability coverage to kick in. As you might guess, attorneys favor this latter coverage, because their one-third or one-half of all the money is a much bigger total. Because billboards are illegal in Alaska, this class of attorneys is forced to advertise on the sides of buses and on late-night TV. *"Have you been in an accident?" "Are you planning to get hurt in an accident?" "Call now, and we'll get you the cash you deserve!"*

A typical evening at a bingo center: Patrons arrive in the late afternoon, and it gets busy around dinner time. The snack bar and the restrooms get crowded but only—and here's the problem—during the breaks between the sets.

Upon entering, patrons buy their bingo cards and borrow their stampers from the cashier. Sets get coupled together, and then there is a longer intermission so the caller can rest their voice. During this time, the patrons grab Mountain Dew, pizza, and popcorn, go outside to smoke, and use the restroom. Females tend to take longer in the restroom than the men, and there generally are more women than men playing bingo. Accordingly, the ladies' restrooms at bingo halls get crowded, with long lines for limited stalls. Then, when the caller's voice intones over the loudspeakers, "Were starting game seven of the evening now," there is a sudden sense of urgency. The players have cards on the table, and those cards aren't going to stamp themselves. The rush is on!

Because money is exchanged—sometimes lots of it—there are surveillance cameras everywhere, except inside the restrooms. I have heard tales of the ladies' rooms becoming chaotic when the bingo caller's voice is heard. Women with legs crossed, pounding on stall doors, others shoving at the sinks, pulling at the paper towel dispensers. And frequently, sink water is sloshed onto the ceramic tile floor.

This typically chaotic scene played out in a serious accident I investigated at an Anchorage bingo center. The carpet had recently been replaced, and the nap and weave of the fabric had not yet been flattened by foot traffic. A 55-year-old woman had stopped at Nordstrom Rack on her way to bingo. The box and tissues of her new cross-trainers were still on the seat of her car when she met up with her girlfriends at the hall. The restroom was crowded at break time, and the woman panicked when she heard the number-calling resume. She dashed out into the room, at which point the brand-new treads on her tennies stuck solidly to the brand-new carpet. She tumbled onto her face and one outstretched arm.

Blood gushed from her broken nose, and one elbow was probably fractured. Nevertheless, the woman didn't cast blame; she saw herself as the one responsible for the accident. If she had just walked, rather than run, she would have been fine. A day later, this woman graciously allowed me to conduct a recorded interview over the phone. Once it was clear that all she needed was help with her medical expenses, I was able to remand the claim file to the insurance company's "premises medical payments" department. The costs would probably exceed the "primary" coverage of the bingo hall, and then her own medical insurance would become "excess" and pay the rest.

On another occasion, at a different Anchorage bingo hall, a woman slipped in front of the restroom sinks. Two other ladies helped her to her feet, and would later become eyewitnesses in this case. I will call the party that slipped Mrs. Hirt; she demanded to speak to the manager, who had already been told of the accident by another patron and was on his way to meet her. Mrs. Hirt claimed that she probably broke her shoulder, so the manager said he'd call 9-1-1. She countered, "No, no, just let me fill out an accident report, and I will stop at a walk-in clinic on the way home."

The bingo hall manager told Mrs. Hirt how sorry he was. He said it was too bad that she would have to leave when she still had un-played cards on the table. As a conciliatory gesture, he told her if she decided to stay, despite her injury, he would have the cashier give her three times the normal number of bingo cards. He gave Mrs. Hirt a second stamper to facilitate the marking of the generous stack of cards laid before her.

The manager then went to the security office and adjusted the three ceiling-mounted surveillance cameras closest to her seat. He made sure they were trained directly on Mrs. Hirt for the rest of the night. The recorders were creating a permanent record, while a cautionary sign on the front door read, "These premises are under video surveillance."

Mrs. Hirt did, in fact, stay until closing. One monitor even captured sweat on her forehead as she bounced from side to side, using both hands to stamp, stamp, stamp. She shrieked "Bingo!" multiple times. The others at her table must have thought she'd gone to bingo-heaven; how did she have so many cards?

In the weeks that followed my initial investigation, Mrs. Hirt didn't answer any of my calls, and no medical bills were submitted to the bingo establishment. It looked as if this potentially ominous case was going away on its own. But no such luck. A three-page letter showed up at my office from one of Anchorage's *personal injury* attorneys. ("Personal injury" is a common misnomer. It should be "bodily injury," because "personal injury" designates libel or slander, but this designation is rarely respected.) The lawyer asserted that Mrs. Hirt had suffered an immediate onset of disablement that fateful evening, and that she had suffered every day and night since. The pain was so severe that she could barely shower or move her right arm above her shoulder. Moreover, mounting doctor and chiropractor bills will follow in the mail to verify the seriousness of her injury on that tragic evening at the bingo hall. Then in the next paragraph, the attorney's tone became pragmatic. Even though Mrs. Hirt's bill might run into six figures, she was a peaceable person who wanted to cause no trouble.

He moved to suggest that instead of drawing this claim out to the lawsuit and litigation stage, which he said Mrs. Hirt would win hands-down, why not consider an alternative? If the insurance company offered a reasonable sum (he didn't say what "reasonable" meant), Mrs. Hirt would sign a release of all claims in his office, and the matter could be put to rest fast. The letter requested that I set up an appointment with him via his secretary, and it said we could discuss the details at his office.

Before calling the attorney, I first confirmed that the videos of Mrs. Hirt had been archived in the bingo hall's security office. Next, I called the attorney's office, bypassing the secretary. I revealed to the lawyer the existence of the videotapes, and I offered to bring copies to his office so we could review them together. I'd even bring a portable VCR if he didn't have one.

Bingo!

He responded that he would check with his secretary and get back to me about the date for my office visit.

Neither the secretary nor the attorney called back. Instead, in the mail a couple days later I received what looked like a boilerplate letter. "Our office no longer represents Mrs. Hirt." I sent that letter to the insurance company and closed my file.

12

All I Want for Christmas

As many as five cruise ships can dock in Ketchikan during high season. Passengers descend en masse onto the eight downtown city blocks. Located on Revillagigedo Island, Ketchikan is scrunched between saltwater and mountains, in many places just a block wide. Across a fjord called the Tongass Narrows lies Ketchikan International Airport, reached by a quaint little ferry. While float planes land near the ferry dock, if you are traveling by jet you hike or drive uphill to the terminal. Two taxiways blasted out of the rock switchback from the gate up higher to the runway, which likewise has been blasted out of the hillside. This gives pilots and passengers the unusual experience of ascending and descending while the wheels are still on the ground. For the pilot up front, this can be a thrill if the corners are icy.

In years past, Ketchikan referred to itself as *The Rain Capital of the World*, but at some point the Ketchikan Convention and Visitors Bureau nixed that. The town's primary sources of pride today are its salmon fishing, its Lingit and Haida (Alaska Natives) heritage, and its unique geographical position along the fabled Inside Passage. As is well-known, in 1867, Congress reluctantly acceded to the recommendation of Secretary of State William Seward to buy Alaska for $7.2 million from Russia. Detractors in Washington, DC, lambasted the Alaska deal as "Seward's Folly" or "Seward's Ice Box."

But Ketchikan's role as *Alaska's First City*, its proud moniker today, came later on. It was cemented during the Klondike Gold Rush that began after huge quantities of the yellow metal were found there in 1896. Voices from Washington, DC, denigrating Seward's purchase suddenly tapered off. Barely seaworthy old ships were pressed into service to bring thousands of prospectors, alongside scoundrels, hooligans, and ladies of the night up from Seattle, Portland, and San Francisco. Every single boatload had to stop in Ketchikan to get processed through U.S. Customs.

Fifteen minutes on foot from the cruise ship docks is Creek Street, which is not a street at all, but a series of boardwalks perched over the mouth of Ketchikan Creek. Spawning salmon splash and mill around below, waiting to ride the next high tide up over the first rapids and eventually lay eggs and die in the same inland valley shallows where they were born.

While it is incredible to see a salmon spawning stream smack dab in the middle of town, the salmon are not the original reason that Creek Street became famous, or infamous, depending on who you ask. Soldiers and seamen supported the burgeoning brothel industry there. Today, those bordellos have been restored to proffer different wares. Local artists including Native woodcarvers produce Alaskan treasures. There are also touristy shops offering saltwater taffy, chocolates, and strong, locally roasted coffee. Among the most popular Ketchikan java labels is "Three Peckered Billy Goat."

Right around the time the calendar flipped over to the year 2000, I interviewed a nonagenarian, a retired Alaskan territorial and state official. He had been involved in a minor Anchorage traffic accident where he wasn't hurt badly. After my work was done, we chatted, and it came to light that I liked Ketchikan, so he told me this story:

> *I was just 17 when I shipped out to Alaska. Life was tough for this kid when I ran away from the*

place I was supposed to call home in Oswego, Oregon. I doubt if anyone noticed that I was gone. I lied about my age and enlisted. I hadn't paid attention in school on the few days when I wasn't truant, so I had no idea where or even what Alaska was. The first clue came when the Army issued me cold-weather boots and a parka. After numerous seasick days, we docked in Ketchikan and had a full week of shore leave.

I was the youngest guy aboard, and hardly able to put up a fight. The other guys urged me to just go do it, and I couldn't admit that I was scared. On Creek Street I lost my virginity to a lip-sticked lady, too old and wrinkly to be sexy. But her eyes, despite the nicotine lines around them, sparkled with kindness. Her gravelly voice mouthed a momma's kindness, which was a balm for this tortured teen; she pulled me in tight to her bosom and somehow at the same time, used her nail-polish fingers to unbutton my shirt and then to do the same with my trousers. I stepped out of my pants and those fingernails scratched my lily-white skin when she pushed my skivvies to the floor. She said she didn't want my money—that's a good thing; I didn't have any.

That afternoon on Creek Street changed me. Was this lady a saint in disguise? Maybe so. After all these years in Alaska, most would agree that I turned out okay.

138

A short mile north of Creek Street on the other side of downtown, at 312 Front Street, there was another institution worth remembering. The false-front structure had been built there sometime before people kept records, and it operated as the Fo'c'sle Bar. From at least the 1930's until it closed in 2003, it was a Ketchikan blue-collar tradition. As logging declined and cruise ships increased, local history lost out. After all, selling diamonds and jade to moneyed tourists off the ships is more profitable than tapping kegs of beer for grimy working-class types.

In 1998, I flew to Ketchikan for a liquor liability claim, the traditional name being a "dram shop claim." My job was usually to unravel the stories of what had happened when drunks wreaked havoc and death. A "dram" is old British for a little shot glass. An English "dram shop," in contrast to a pub, was set up to sell hard liquor by the drink.

Until recent decades, floating logging camps were anchored in bays off the islands to the west of Ketchikan. Once a month, the loggers would get a free weekend and go to Ketchikan by skiff or float plane. Cleverly, and pushing the boundaries of ethics, the Fo'c'sle Bar encouraged loggers to use the bar's address, 312 Front St. Ketchikan, AK, 99901, as their own mailing address. Below the neon *Alaskan Amber* sign on the south wall inside, mailboxes labeled from A to Z held loggers' letters and cards from home, alongside demands for child support payments, and other blue-collar correspondence.

On days when loggers were expected in town, the Fo'c'sle's manager would head to the National Bank of Alaska to grab enough fives, tens, twenties, and fifties to cash their hard-earned paychecks. This suited the fellows, who would usually arrive around dinner time after the bank had closed. In a flash, after signing over their paychecks to the Fo'c'sle, they had wallets full of cash.

The Fo'c'sle sold hamburgers and fries that could be washed down with beer. There was no alcohol in the logging camps, and plenty of it was soon buzzing through the collective heads of these young and hardy fellows. What next? Darts? Pool? More beer. I'll buy beer and shots for everyone! First round's on me! Next one's on you, and you and then you! By 3 AM closing time, the amount of cash that had passed through their wallets and back into the Fo'c'sle's cash register was, ahem, staggering.

The Fo'c'sle had three pool tables. A 26-year-old man from a camp on Prince of Wales Island I'll call him Bruce—had taken the 25-minute float plane ride to the Ketchikan dock. As he confessed when I met him the following Tuesday, all that Alaskan Amber had made him think he was a pool shark. By midnight, Bruce told me, he had lost track of who played and who won. No matter. Another beer and another shot of whiskey should do.

He leaned on the bar and blathered his order to the bartender, and then with a fresh beer in hand, he turned toward a pool table. But his legs had already called it a night. Bruce plunged headlong onto the mahogany edge of the first pool table. His teeth cracked hard on the rail, and he crumpled onto the spruce-plank flooring, beer soaking his shirt. He rolled underneath the pool table, but amid the gloom and noise of the jukebox, none of the other drunks even noticed. Bleeding from a lacerated upper lip, he vomited out some of the night's booze along with his upper two front teeth onto the spruce boards. Finally, Bruce got up and made his way to the bathroom, where he stuffed toilet paper into the holes where his teeth had been. Before he staggered out the door, the bartender got his name and filled out an accident report, which the owner would see first thing in the morning. Bruce still had to make it back to the well-used bed in the room he'd rented, a two-block journey punctuated by stumbling and bumping into doorways along a deserted Front Street.

Saturday was tough for Bruce, but by Sunday he felt like he could maybe look some sunny-side-up eggs in the eyes, if he could just figure out a way to slide them past his aching jaw and into his still churning belly.

141

First thing on Saturday, the Fo'c'sle manager reported the incident via their Ketchikan insurance agent's emergency line. In Anchorage on Monday, I got the assignment and set plans to fly to Ketchikan on Tuesday morning. The Fo'c'sle, like other bars, had limited, no-fault medical payments insurance coverage for anybody who was hurt on premises. Still, the insurance company feared that Bruce might get connected with one of the many hungry lawyers and start a classic dram shop claim, suing the bar for knowingly serving liquor to a drunk patron, something highly illegal but commonplace. I had already seen the ways that a well-prosecuted dram shop claim could buy an attorney and his girlfriend a couple months in Puerto Vallarta.

But the bar and its insurer were in luck. Bruce was so humiliated that he didn't want money; he just wished he could turn back the clock and have stayed in camp that weekend. But he still needed to do something about his two front teeth. Butterfly-shaped Band-Aids from the drugstore had helped his lip scab together well enough, though it definitely should have been sutured at the hospital. Bruce's biggest concern, however, was how he was ever going to get a girlfriend; he'd never be able to smile at a girl again, he lamented.

In a stroke of good luck, I found a dental office that also did orthodontics just a couple blocks from the Fo'c'sle. Bruce went in and got a binding estimate of the price for the orthodontia, along with a couple of other fillings thrown in. The insurance company wanted me to provide a notarized release of all claims for the final amount they'd pay for Bruce. The dental office agreed to a small contingency supplement so that they could guarantee the price of their services in advance. Bruce was thrilled with the arrangement, even though it would mean multiple trips back and forth between the logging camp and Ketchikan, where he would hopefully choose to steer clear of the Fo'c'sle.

When the settlement check arrived in my office the week before the Christmas holiday, I had other work in Ketchikan, so on Christmas Eve, I met with Bruce. He flashed me a toothless smile, and we drove to the bank together to sign over the check that would help him get back on his feet.

Spike Jones and His City Slickers first came out with the song *All I Want for Christmas Is My Two Front Teeth*, and later *Alvin and the Chipmunks* made it popular with TV audiences. I asked Bruce if he knew about the song. He said yes, he remembered his parents having the *Christmas with the Chipmunks* LP as a kid. The poetry of the moment wasn't lost on Bruce that Christmas Eve.

13
Scalded

I'll nickname her Val—short for "Valiant." She was born a paraplegic in North Carolina, but from childhood she dreamed of wilderness rivers and mountains in Alaska. Val knew she'd see life from a wheelchair, but she was determined that her mobility device would not keep her from her dreams. She had no feeling in her emaciated legs below the cauda equina at the base of her spine. Extreme caution was necessary around flames, razors, knives, and even pins. If, for example, she cut her leg while shaving, she would only know it when she saw the blood on the linoleum.

She graduated with honors from Stanford, and then answered the call of the North. With her educational credentials, Val was a shoo-in for a supervisory position with the Alaska Department of Health and Social Services (DHSS). Her professional focus lay naturally in helping the physically disabled. Her job mandated that she travel to Alaskan communities from Ketchikan in the Panhandle to Utkiaġvik on the Arctic Ocean.

The 1990 *Americans with Disabilities Act* was on the horizon, but even that piece of legislation would take years to make it easier for Val to get in and out of aircraft. If Val took the flight to Kotzebue, for example, a ramp worker would fold up her wheelchair and put it in the baggage hold, and then another might carry her across the tarmac and up the stairs either belted into a narrow chair or on his back. This was the type of indignity that she accepted.

In Anchorage, Val used the city buses. During the summer, the fold-out wheelchair ramp made it possible to get in the door, but when it was snowy and icy, the task became nearly overwhelming. A municipal van service helped a lot, and colleagues from work gave her rides.

Then over time, Val's back pain, which she thought was probably just from sitting too much, turned out to be liver cancer. It is impossible in a few sentences to summarize the extent of her suffering and treatments over the next two years. The DHSS gave Val extended medical leave for cancer treatments Outside. For Alaskans, that term means the Lower 48 states. Her medical care was in Seattle and San Francisco.

Similar to Val's school and college years, she was able to beat the odds stacked overwhelmingly against her. She returned to being the same independent, full-time DHSS supervisor in Anchorage. With practice, she became adept at navigating ice on sidewalks and getting in and out of her apartment on her own. Her place had beautiful views of Cook Inlet from one window, while in the winters the ice-skaters of Westchester Lagoon could be seen from another. People who knew Val described her with adjectives such as indefatigable and unsinkable. After her treatments in the Lower 48, life for her returned to relative normalcy, and stayed that way for eight more years.

Then the cancer returned. Val went back to Seattle for treatment, but this time the nauseating and strength-robbing treatments didn't grant her remediation. While she felt fairly good, the doctors explained that their efforts only provided her some extra comfort during the limited time she had left. While nobody had a crystal ball, doctors told her she only had about a year and a half left to live.

Elbert Hubbard wrote, "When life gives you lemons, make lemonade." Val asked her mom if she would come up to Alaska from North Carolina and move in to help her, not to prepare to die, but to live her last months as fully as she could. After Mom arrived, the two of them hit upon an idea. That coming summer, they would organize a family reunion of roughly 15 people on a river in the Carolinas. This would be no potato salad and hot dogs picnic, but a three-day rafting trip run by an outfitter. One of the rafts would be equipped with a special seat for Val. It would be elevated, and she fancied that it would appear a bit like her holding court over her subjects, all relatives and friends.

Although Anchorage was still covered in snow and ice in early spring that year, planning for the summer reunion was well under way. Val had been granted early retirement after what must have been the biggest going-away party in her office's history.

Unfortunately, Val would suffer additional tragedy—which is how I learned of her story. The maintenance man, in charge of the three-building complex where Val lived, got fired. In a fury he determined to get revenge on the property management company. Gas-fired hot water heaters can explode if the safety is disabled and the temperature set past the red-line maximum. That is exactly what he did to the units in all three basements. In addition, he disabled the backflow protectors so hot water flowed from both the hot and cold taps in the entire building.

Fortunately, the water heaters' relief valves worked, so there were no explosions, but scalding water was sent to every faucet in the complex. As would be discovered later, the saboteur had thrown away his work keys and left Anchorage; the police surmised he had probably flown to the Lower 48.

For her morning bath, Mom helped Val onto the shower seat in the bathtub as usual, and then she pulled the curtain and left Val to enjoy her morning spa routine. She expected Val to call her when she was finished. Val had turned the water-dial to medium and pulled the telephone shower head toward her torso, but the water was scalding hot, so she screamed and dropped the nozzle to the floor of the tub. The water spray continued; both of Val's feet were scalded, but she felt nothing. Mom heard the initial scream and came fast. She turned off the water and helped Val out of the tub, finding nothing but scalding hot water coming out no matter which direction she turned the dial. When she called the property management company to report the problem, she learned that others had already done the same.

For Val, nothing appeared to be amiss at first, but in short time her feet turned cherry red. Over the next hours, the skin began to blister severely. After a 9-1-1 call, EMTs transported Val to the emergency burn unit at an Anchorage hospital, where she ended up spending several weeks. Then Mom rented a hospital bed so Val could come home, where she remained flat at all times with her feet suspended from pulleys. A visiting nurse checked in daily and changed her bandages as necessary.

Val lay flat, with her mother in a chair by her side, while I conducted my recorded interview about this tragic occurrence. I was working on behalf of the insurer of the apartment complex, and this was by no means a "one-two-three" interview. Val started her story recounting her childhood as a paraplegic. She went step by step through each phase until the last, including the unexpected cancellation of the coming summer's river rafting extravaganza.

As I recall it through my own tears, Val said, "I was okay with paraplegia, okay in high school, okay at Stanford, okay with cancer, okay with cancer again, okay with the idea of dying, but I just don't have it in me to be okay another time."

The investigation into the accident was easy. This was going to be a bodily injury liability claim on the property owner's insurance policy. The managers of the apartments, too, expressed their sorrow about what happened. The Anchorage Police Department's detectives were involved, and the last I heard a warrant was out for the arrest of the former maintenance man, who had become a fugitive on the lam.

For the first couple of months, the burn specialists worried about infection, but daily treatments and antibiotics did their jobs. Val ended up needing a special gurney to transport her to the hospital for follow-up treatments.

Once again, Val the Valiant proved the naysayers wrong. She recovered astonishingly well from her burns, and by October one could hardly tell that her feet had been burned so badly. Mom stayed with Val while the deep snow made Anchorage white again.

As expected, Val died that winter.

Pacific Trillium found in the forests of the Pacific Northwest and Southeast Alaska. Usually a symbol of hope, sometimes of mourning.

14

Topless

I was the only adjuster at Wilton Adjustment Service who could handle dram shop liability claims. It wasn't that my colleagues couldn't do the work, but that their wives wouldn't stand for their husbands setting foot in topless bars. Although I considered these men's spouses to be generally well-balanced individuals, I found their insecurity startling. I, however, reaped the benefit. All of the liquor liability claims in Southeast, Southcentral, and Western Alaska ended up on my desk, and in Dudley Do-Right innocence, I thoroughly enjoyed the work.

I recall one fatality on the roadway in front of a now defunct bar called the "Borealis Beach Club," located on the Parks Highway outside Wasilla. I had arranged to interview a dancer in her early twenties there during the 7 PM to close shift. On the night of the interview, she stepped down from the stage, and we went to a booth in the back of the club where I had prepared some documents and my voice recorder.

The tragedy had occurred two nights before my interview. The dancer's older brother had come to the club just to hang out with his little sister. He was despondent about his girlfriend, and his depression was possibly compounded by drugs. He stayed later and later, never outwardly drunk, but nursing one beer after another. This factor is where the potential of a liquor liability claim for overservice of alcohol against the Borealis Beach Club entered the story.

Little sister was on stage when she saw big brother bolt out the front door of the bar. The only possible destination appeared to be the convenience mart across the highway. Maybe he wanted to buy some food there, or maybe he was tired of living. A couple minutes later, a commotion outside was followed 10 minutes later by police and fire truck sirens. Her brother had been struck and instantly killed by a southbound car.

As far as a liquor liability claim, the toxicology test of the corpse showed he was indeed intoxicated. However, owing to his sister's honesty about his controlled consumption during the night, and about his state of mind at the time of death, it seemed unlikely that a dram shop claim would arise. One never did. The only physical damage in the accident was a body-shaped indentation on the grille and hood of car that struck him. That type of damage would be paid by the driver's insurance policy under "comprehensive" coverage. But there would never be any compensation to the driver for the nightmare-inducing shock of seeing a young man die in front of him on his windshield.

When the young dancer came down from the stage to be interviewed, she didn't see it necessary to change her get-up. The top of her costume was designed to be pulled off in a single move and had less fabric than the handkerchief in the back pocket of my Levi's. Whenever she sighed, either the left or right breast popped out. In wiggling to adjust one side to cover up, she invariably caused the other breast to work its way out. I pretended not to notice. I felt helpless with nothing to say to comfort her. I suppose that maybe it was therapeutic for her to tell me her story. She also expressed grief about the emotional suffering of the driver that struck and killed her brother.

After pressing the stop button my recorder, I thanked her and wished her well under the horrible circumstances. It was difficult to imagine her returning to get dollar bills stuck into her bikini that evening. But her line of work was an unforgiving one. There was no paid leave. If you didn't work, you didn't pay the rent.

In order to conduct investigations at bars, I adjusted my work schedule to match their nightly routines. When I walked in the door, the dancers and servers rarely noticed my briefcase, so they smiled and showed me to a seat, leaning over me purposefully so that it was tough not to stare. Sometimes it took a while for the manager to come out from the office to meet me, so I just whiled away my time among the other spectators. Despite the fact that I told them I wasn't there to place a bar order, the girls persisted. They feigned sexual attraction—because that was their job.

One time, and one time only, a dancer was successful in giving me a no-touching-allowed lap dance. She was in her thirties, and up close I saw that she had stretch marks. Like other moms around the world, she was making a living. Yet, because of her good luck in the gene-pool lottery, instead of mopping office floors, she had a means to make better money. For me, that lap dance was colossally awkward, and I was counting the seconds until it was over. I tipped her, and she went on to another fellow.

One of the most popular topless venues in Anchorage is still *The Crazy Horse*, run by two proper and congenial ladies. If you ran into them at a charity luncheon, you would never imagine that they ran a gentlemen's club. These two women were admirably protective of "their girls." They hired strong, young men as bouncers, not just to guard the entry, but to make certain that no customer touched the dancers or servers except when they went up front to slip ones and fives into their tanga bottoms.

The owners' rule was, "Don't work the pole upside down, and certainly do not oil up your skin before you use the pole!" Did the girls pay attention to these ladies? No, they knew that the guys in the audience hooted and hollered when they did wild acrobatic moves. I was there to investigate what happened to one of these dancers. She was oiled up to a sheen and first did several dance moves around the stage to pulsating music. Then she ran and leaped for the pole, a move which was supposed to end in an upside-down twirl, her legs forming a V in the air. Instead, she made it through the first half of the maneuver only to lose her grip and land head-first on a table in the front row. It was unclear if the fellow sitting there had been planning to slip dollar bills into her bikini bottom, but despite the discomfort of the beer sloshed into his lap, he got more skin-to-skin contact with a dancer than he could have hoped for that night.

This became an insurance investigation because the worker's compensation insurance carrier doubted the story in the loss report. How could a young woman need chiropractic treatments after dancing in a topless club? They suspected that perhaps she had actually been in an auto accident or even beaten by her boyfriend—as too often happens with dancers. So, I was sent to interview those involved.

When I got back to the office the next morning, the ladies of the secretarial pool were a-twitter. "Oh, Kristian, was that investigation last night distracting? Did you have a tough time concentrating on your work?" I responded, "You have no idea!" You see, because of the sensitive nature of the claim, a bouncer accompanied me to all three interviews that night. Then it came time for me to go into the security office and interview him about what he had seen. I recall a poster on the doorway advertising "Honey Melons," a dancer coming up from the Lower 48 the next week. By the photo I could barely fathom how much silicone was in her body. But this bouncer was a 26-year-old blue-eyed guy crowned with a mop of curly blond hair. He was a 6-feet-four compaction of pecs, biceps, triceps, and quadriceps in a lycra T-shirt, with a smile that never left his lips.

I started my recorder to get his witness statement and began with the usual identifying information and acknowledgment the conversation was being recorded. Then I looked at his eyes, and I am not sure what happened. The recorder was running, but I hadn't heard a word he said. I had no idea at that point how to ask follow-up questions because my mind was lost in his smile. I wiggled my way out of the problem by saying, "Your testimony is so important that I would like for you to go through it once more. Please start at the beginning, and I will take detailed notes." For nine and a half minutes I succeeded in keeping my eyes on my note pad.

The girls in the office didn't yet know about me what I am sure the bouncer understood within a couple minutes. They say that homosexuals have "gaydar," and I am guessing that this too-perfectly toned young man had a gaydar apparatus that was beeping pretty loudly during that interview.

My work finished, I went home. The next day I prepared my report to explain to the company that everything about the loss report was legitimate. Her claim for chiropractic treatment and physical therapy was covered through Crazy Horse's workers' compensation insurance policy. I wondered if the dancer would be in good enough shape after treatment to return to work at the club. No doubt, she would if she could. Where else could a young woman with no education make a decent living, to say nothing of being ogled at by horny men happy to give her their telephone numbers for "supplemental" work on the side?

15

Who Is Your Mother?

It was February. My briefcase was in my left gloved-hand, while my other hand steadied me as I descended a couple steps out of the Cessna Caravan. I had flown from Bethel to Chevak via Hooper Bay. As I inhaled my first breath, I coughed; I knew from experience this reaction to one's first breath meant the air temperature was at least -20° Fahrenheit. If in the next few moments I felt the hairs inside my nose freeze and pinch, that meant the air I breathed was at least 30° below zero. Small aircraft can operate at temperatures as low as -59° F, assuming that the plane starts its engines in a warm hangar, or with piles of blankets over the cowling and a warming fire underneath.

All of this coughing and pinching business wasn't the least bit scientific, but it worked for me. By the way, for those who think in Celsius, remember that at -40°, the world's two temperature scales converge. Whether you are using Celsius in Norway or Fahrenheit in Alaska, forty below zero is cold. Below that, it's just better to stay inside and stay away from cracks around windows and doors. In my travels, I had found that when it was minus 40° to minus 60°, even when I was wearing my ultra-insulated parka, the cold would find the seams and penetrate so deeply I could feel a sting along the back of my arms where the cold passed through both the parka and my Pendleton wool shirt.

Based on my various measurement strategies, I guessed it was -28° F in Chevak that day. After stepping out of the plane, I walked across the ice and into this comparatively large (about 900 residents) Cup'ik Eskimo village. I had come to investigate an accident at the school that had happened that past September, when liquid water was still to be found outdoors.

School was in session, so I went to the office and registered for a "visitor's lunch" in the cafeteria. The Chevak School is the main structure in the Kashunamiut School District and has 350 students. I thought it was pretty cool that my lunch ticket allowed me to eat with

162

the kindergarten through sixth-grade kids. The meal was a multi-bean soup with pilot bread and a canned fruit cocktail. There are no restaurants in Chevak—in fact, I don't know of any Alaskan community off the road system except for Aniak that has one. The two alternatives to being lucky enough to snag a visitor's lunch at the school are: 1) Buy beef jerky, Pop Tarts, and Pepsi at the village store, or 2) Call ahead to find people willing to take you in and feed you. If you are "eating Native," lunch might mean a seal steak or a caribou roast or salmon.

Because Chevak is a larger village with an airport that has runway lights, it is possible to do a one-day trip in the winter. My plan was to be back in Bethel to catch the evening Alaska Airlines jet home to Anchorage. However, if the investigation went long, that wouldn't be a problem, because I could overnight on the tumbling mats in the school's gym, or if my luck were good, be given use of one of the apartments for Kashunamiut School District VIPs such as public health nurses and special education teachers.

My investigation went fast. A couple of second-graders were involved in an accident that was all but inevitable for youngsters. There were a half a dozen enormous diesel tanks that made up the school's *tank farm*. They had been upgraded for safety and environmental security. Instead of just being out in the open in front of the school building as they had been for years, they were made "safer" by enclosing them. First, a ditch was excavated around the whole tank farm, and it was lined with heavy-grade plastic sheeting, a moat to catch any spilled oil. No oil leaked, but it quickly filled with rainwater, a place for kids to run their toy boats in circles around the tanks. Eventually, a 10-foot-high chain link fence was erected around the moat to prevent kids from accidentally drowning.

Anybody who knows children can guess what happened next. These Cup'ik kids used their climbing skills to ascend the fence, dropping down into the area beside the moat on the other side to continue to sail their carved, toy boats. Going home after play time was a repeat, climb and drop. The ascent of the fence was pretty easy, but climbing over the top and grasping the wire loops for the down-climb was tougher. Often the kids just jumped or fell. Ten feet is a long way to fall and not get injured.

Inevitably, a kid broke his arm near the wrist while jumping down off the tank farm fence, and the parents got a Bethel attorney to present a claim for damages. The medical claim was a bit more involved than one might expect because the fracture impinged on a growth plate, meaning if the growth was stunted, the child might need to undergo multiple surgeries in the future to make sure both arms were of the same length when he grew up. My investigation at the behest of the insurer representing the Kashunamiut School

District revealed that an attorney could allege and probably prove in court that the high chain-link fence was an "attractive nuisance." The school would need to do something to keep such accidents from happening again and again. While I wasn't in on the discussions regarding the remediation of the problem, it was going to be tough for the school district to find a kid-proof solution short of razor wire on top, or snapping guard dogs inside the fence.

When it came time for lunch in Chevak that day, I observed a cultural phenomenon that the kids themselves probably weren't aware of. Each of the roughly two dozen elementary age kids in my area came to make introductions. One by one, they lined up to shake my hand, and each of the youngest ones asked me my name and, "Who is your mother?" I responded, "Thelma Longmire," which satisfied them even though they had never heard of her.

I had engaged a tutor in Western Alaskan Yup'ik. This is the first language of most Alaska Natives in this part of the state, along with the sister tongues of Cup'ik (roughly pronounced "choo-pick"), which is spoken in Chevak and Hooper Bay, as well as a variant, Siberian Yup'ik, spoken on Saint Lawrence Island and in Siberia. In order to initiate a conversation in Yup'ik, you must first establish your familial relationship, as that affects the choice of words and their prefixes, bases, and post-bases. One's lineage runs through the mother. And in

165

these children asking for my mother's name they were following thousands of years of tradition.

Native kids are loved, and they know they enjoy a special role in Native society. Toys are big business in the commercial centers of Dillingham, Bethel, Unalakleet, Nome, Kotzebue, and Utkiaġvik, because moms and dads lavish gifts on their children. When I have visited Moravian church services—the Alaska headquarters is in Bethel—I have been impressed by how the children have free reign to visit all over the church during the singing. But when it's time to be respectful, they are quiet, incredibly quiet, and still. When an elder is speaking, nobody interrupts.

So, this brings me to the Lutheran church in Nome. During a weekend stay-over, my previously mentioned friend and gold-miner's daughter, June Engstrom, took me to the Nome Lutheran Church on a Sunday morning. The regular pastor wasn't there, so a retired fill-in minister from Seattle took over the service. It was the typical Lutheran liturgy until...

The pastor invited all the children, all Native kids, young Inupiaq and Yup'ik Eskimos, to come up to the front of the church and be seated on the carpet in a semi-circle around him while he acted out an animated story. His talent as a storyteller would get the kids involved, right? Right? Unfortunately, nobody explained Native ways to this visiting minister. While Native kids can be as boisterous on the playground as any of their counterparts around the world, these children learn respect for adults and for strangers. A quiet demeanor around one's elders is fundamental.

When the pastor started in on the New Testament parable of the Good Shepherd, he didn't anticipate having a silent audience. As the story goes, the shepherd has 100 sheep, but when one gets lost, he is willing to leave the 99 in search of the one. The pastor gyrated from side to side and pointed to the imaginary hill where the lost sheep must be, but the kids sat motionless like little statues. Realizing he had a "tough crowd" on his hands, he laid into the performance even harder. Finally, it occurred to him that maybe the kids didn't even know what a sheep was.

"Do you know what a sheep is? Raise your hand." No movement. Finally, he called on one girl, who simply shrugged her shoulders. The pastor decided to attempt an explanation, saying, "A sheep is like a sled dog." The problem is that while the size might be close, the demeanor of Siberian Huskies and Malemutes is nothing at all like a timid sheep. Every village child learns that the dog yards, with their howling and jumping canines are danger zones. Never, ever cross through one! Children are told stories by Mom and Dad and Grandpa and

Grandma of other children maimed and even killed by sled dogs.

Even after his sheep and Husky analogy, the kids remained silent. Still, the determined pastor pressed on with the story. "One sheep is off in the rocky hills, bleating for its mom. The little sheep is cold. It is crying."

Then the pastor asked the kids, "So, do you know what happens next? Someone cares so much about that sheep that he leaves all the others and goes out into the dark to find the little lost lamb, er, sheep. And do you know who that man is?"

Silence.

Again, he asks, "Who goes after the lost sheep?"

Silence.

"Who will go after the poor lost one?"

A little boy raised his hand, and a greatly relieved expression crossed the pastor's face. He pointed to the boy, and the small voice asked proudly, *"The hunter?"*

16

He Just Lost His Head

The name *Parks Highway* is confusing. The route leads to both Denali National Park and Denali State Park, but that is coincidence. The Parks was completed in 1971 as the *Anchorage to Fairbanks Highway*, but it was quickly renamed the George Parks Highway to honor the man who was Alaska Territorial Governor from 1925 to 1933. While it is an exaggeration to say civil war was averted through this naming decision, the rivalry between Alaska's first and second-largest cities meant the fight would likely not have been pretty if the original name had stuck as the "Anchorage to Fairbanks" and not the "Fairbanks to Anchorage."

The Parks is crucial to transport and commerce, but its costs in lives of people, moose, and bears is gruesome. Before it was constructed, the way from north to south was via the Alcan (called the Alaska Highway today), then the Richardson, and finally the Glenn. In winter, the journey could take two days. But weather wasn't the only limiting factor. In 1920, when the Richardson was built, engineers from the Lower 48 didn't know about permafrost. The lenses of ice in the ground that periodically swelled and collapsed made this "America's safest highway," because if you drove faster than 20 MPH, the frost heaves would cause your skull to ricochet off the headliner of your car again and again. Today, even after a hundred years of rebuilding, the Richardson is still a roller coaster ride.

The Parks Highway, on the other hand, with its long straightaways and banked curves, cut the trip-time between Fairbanks and Anchorage to less than six hours. If there were an Olympics for the bloodiest of long-haul highways in Alaska, the Parks, the Seward, and the Glenn would all be on the podium, but the Parks would surely get the gold. To illustrate: About 1999, a 26-year-old airman from Eielson Air Force Base at North Pole, near Fairbanks, was speeding south in his Toyota Corolla. It slid—apparently on a patch of ice—into the path of a northbound semi.

He Just Lost His Head

The head-on collision scattered metal, bones, organs, and clothing across the snow for hundreds of feet in all directions. Within hours, ravens, wolves, and even squirrels were feasting. The Corolla's body panels were units of red and black that contrasted with the snow. The double-trailer semi was mostly intact, but it carved a ditch 50 feet long through the snow to the east. Sam Weatherford, our heavy-equipment and truck physical damage expert, was on scene the next day. He walked out into the deep snow to get panoramic photos of the accident's aftermath. Something crunched beneath one of Sam's boots, and he looked down to see an eight-inch-long segment of vertebrae from the airman's spine.

By the time I retired, I had written many ghastly-gruesome reports to attorneys and insurance companies about accidents on the Parks. One of them involved two Fairbanks high school lovebirds, which reminded me how hormone-driven teenagers need divine intervention just to stay alive. In this story, however, it looks like these two kids' guardian angels clocked out early that day.

Winter in Fairbanks, Alaska's *Golden Heart City*, is long, dark, and very cold—minus 20° to minus 40° is common. When high school and university spring break comes, kids borrow Mom's SUV—in this instance it was a Nissan Pathfinder—and head south for a week of thawing out in the Anchorage tropics, where daytime temperatures in the spring rise above freezing.

Two high school seniors were in the Pathfinder. At the wheel was a young man, and in the passenger seat beside him was his fiancée. The guy had been planning on doing two years of mission work for his church before starting college, and his sweetheart promised she'd stay faithful until he got back.

It was cold in the north, but the Parks was mostly free of snow and ice, a perfect day to cruise down to Anchorage while testing the limits of the Pathfinder's speedometer. According to the eyewitness whose story follows, things were getting "frisky" by the time they passed Willow, on the southern third of the route.

That witness was a 36-year-old man from Girdwood, a Mount Alyeska ski aficionado, driving a White-Freightliner cabover semi. He was also towing an old mobile home from a condemned trailer park that had been picked as the site of an Anchorage office tower. The destination of this extra-long single wide was a plot of land in an Alaskan version of the Ozarks near Trapper Creek. One could buy a used trailer cheaply in Anchorage, then aside from drilling a well, the only significant cost would be getting the unit hauled up the Parks Highway and set on concrete blocks. This was the late 1990's. The single-wides, at 14-feet, were exactly the same width of a lane in the older and narrower section of the Parks Highway. The trailer itself was wider than the White-Freightliner's cab. As the mobile home had a rusty undercarriage and flat tires, it was sitting up high on a temporary carriage in order to be hauled, so it was now significantly taller than it had been when it was sitting in the Anchorage trailer park.

On that afternoon near Willow, the northbound White-Freightliner driver was traveling with the requisite pilot cars both in front and in back. The car about a hundred yards ahead of him bore flashing yellow lights and a big sign: WIDE LOAD. The truck driver struggled—but was mostly successful at—keeping the trailer between the center stripe and the fog line of his northbound lane. As told to me in our interview, after passing the cutoff to Talkeetna he had remarked to himself, "It is uncanny how with me sitting up so high and with the sun directly behind me this afternoon, I can see clearly down into the front seats of each of the oncoming cars."

He suddenly pulled his foot off the accelerator when he glimpsed the kids' white SUV nearly sideswipe the front pilot car. He laid on the horn and grabbed the wheel harder while he braked. He couldn't panic-stop because that would certainly throw the truck and trailer into a skid across both lanes. The Pathfinder was now aimed at the White-Freightliner's front bumper. Where was the Pathfinder's driver? He could not see anybody behind the wheel, but he could see that the passenger, a young woman, was sitting upright with her eyes closed. After his air horn sounded, she opened her eyes and threw up her hands. The driver then popped up behind the steering wheel, and he threw the wheel of the Pathfinder to the right. That course correction almost saved them.

The Pathfinder's left side scraped along the driver's side of the cabover truck. But then in what the truck driver described as the most sickening crunching of metal he had ever heard, the leading edge of the double-wide peeled off the left-hand half of the Nissan's roof all the way from the windshield to the tailgate. In an instant, the boy's head and neck were gone.

The White-Freightliner coasted to a stop up the road and the drivers of both pilot cars came running. Stationed in nearby Talkeetna, Alaska State Troopers and EMTs were on the scene in minutes. Traffic on the Parks was blocked both northbound and southbound until after midnight.

From the Trooper's report, I learned that the female passenger was conscious, sitting in the passenger seat, but unable to move when he arrived on the scene. The paramedics found no physical injury that would make her immobile. They loaded her onto a gurney and wheeled her into the aid vehicle. Her diagnosed bodily injuries were superficial lacerations and fragments of windshield glass embedded in her skin. After she regained her composure a tiny bit in the aid car with the doors open, she told the Trooper her story. She knew nothing of what happened because she had been sleeping. She awoke when the windshield exploded. The Trooper wrote one telling line in his report, though. When he approached the wrecked Pathfinder, the young woman's jeans and panties were down around her ankles.

A medical examiner's vehicle had been dispatched from Anchorage to handle what was left of the boy's body. Before the Parks Highway could be reopened again, the staff would need to certify for the Troopers that they had loaded up the torso and conducted a diligent search for missing body parts. The remains were taken to Anchorage for toxicological and forensic analysis.

Out of respect for the sensibilities of the White-Freightliner's driver, I waited two days to interview him about the accident. He was back home at his cabin at the foot of Mount Alyeska, but he suggested we could meet for coffee and the interview at New Sagaya market in Midtown Anchorage, 42 miles away. It was a beautiful early spring day with ice flows rolling in the tide on Turnagain Arm. He arrived late and apologized for his tardiness, explaining that he had chosen to ride his mountain bike because when he went out to his car, he was unable to put himself behind the wheel. I

175

told him that I certainly could have driven down to Girdwood to meet him, but he said no, he felt that the bike ride on that gorgeous Alaskan day would clear his mental fog. After a cordial interview, he mounted his bike and wondered aloud how many months he'd need before he could drive a semi again.

The insurance company told the attorney to whom I was reporting to put my investigation into abeyance for a year, and if there were no further activity, to archive it for an additional seven years plus the length of time it would take the young minor to reach the age of legal majority. As is usual in fatalities, the insurance company's management okayed the decision not to present a claim to the driver's estate (in this case, his parents) for reimbursement of the repairs to the White-Freightliner. The leading corner of the trailer sustained only minor damage, so that wasn't a factor. However, the insurance company instructed the defense attorney that if anyone attempted to pursue a negligence claim against the semi driver, the attorney was to reopen the file and vigorously defend him.

For the sake of the parents and relatives of both the boy and the girl, everyone on our side of the claim hoped they would never have to find out about the girl's panties, even though that was unlikely, as they had probably also read the Troopers' report. Many times, I thought about the girl herself. I hoped that she was able to find a minister or a counselor to help her to understand that she wasn't responsible for her boyfriend's death. That is the way the case ended.

17

Fragments in a Body Bag

Kodiak is the largest of Alaska's 1,800 named islands. The word Kodiak also designates the local subspecies of grizzly bears that can stand 10 feet tall on their hind legs. The biggest town on Kodiak is also called Kodiak. It is one hour from Anchorage on an Alaska Airlines jet, and from the airport you can take a scheduled or chartered fixed-wheel bush planes to a host of remote villages. Alternatively, if your final destination entails a water landing, you head to a float plane base on a lake in the middle of town. If you are determined to go by car, it is a four-and-a-half-hour drive from Anchorage to Homer, and then 15 hours on a ferry that sails three times a week from the Alaska Marine Highway terminal on the Homer Spit in Kachemak Bay.

Kodiak's ultra-green mountains dropping into the sea look like an incarnation of the mythological Elysian Fields. Mostly, the island is too rugged and steep for roads, so settlements are positioned in or near coves or bays where supply ships arrive a couple times a year. Every village on Kodiak and on nearby Afognak Island has either seaplane access or a gravel runway for wheeled aircraft.

One such seaplane and summer-barge-only village has a dozen houses spread for miles along a cove. During fall rains, the creeks on the mountainside above the settlement transport immense burdens of sand, rocks, and boulders to the sea. The problem is that those water corridors carry so much detritus that they regularly clog up, causing the creeks to overflow and seek new channels. This is a frequent problem in cases where a person's homestead lies near such a creek, of which there are scores flowing into the sea.

One man, some would call him a hermit because he lived so far from civilization, was a 40-year resident of the settlement in question. A creek, which used to run near his cabin, had taken a turn on the flank of the mountain above his place, and he feared that in the coming rainy month of October, the water would find its way to his kitchen door.

The nearest neighbor (1 mile away) had an ancient road grader and a Caterpillar bulldozer-tractor with an eight-foot blade on the front. The Caterpillar's engine moved two big, metal lugs or tracks, similar to those seen on tanks of war. As a neighborly gesture, the owner offered to lend the man the machine as he had in the past so that the homesteader could carve out a new creek bed and construct a rock wall that would force the creek away from his house. The owner cautioned him that the rig was getting old and cranky, not unlike both of them, and that the engine cut out from time to time. This would prove to happen every few minutes, especially when the dozer sat at an uphill angle, which, in this operation was most of the time.

Re-channeling the creek bed and building a rock wall was going to be a three-day project if all went well, but because of the engine problems, it was slow-going. The first day went okay, with the engine only cutting out now and then. During the next day, it became more than a mere aggravation, as he related to the owner over the radio-phone during his nightly call. After some tinkering, he discovered that it was a problem with old wiring that could be temporarily fixed by jiggling this and pulling that. On the third and final day of the project, the engine cut out constantly.

The rest of this story is a logical reconstruction, as there was no radio call to the owner on the third night. In the Caterpillar's cab, the operator's seat, ignition, and other controls were covered by a metal canopy situated behind the engine, with its massive radiator located up front by the blade. On both sides of the driver's seat, the tracks were covered with steel cowlings, meaning the operator could get in and out of the cab without having to step on the lugs of the steel track. There were roughly six inches of clearance between the cowlings and the roller tracks on both sides.

On the third day, the bulldozer was pointed up the slope, the engine apparently dying repeatedly. In this situation, any human would become irritated to the point of distraction, and this could be what caused the operator to lose sight of caution, jumping out on the right side to jiggle the spark plugs and kick the engine again. To ensure the stationary bulldozer stayed that way, he kept it in gear. It was in reverse.

The man evidently stepped off the right cowling and knelt on the treads by the engine, where he could wiggle the wiring. That meant that his left boot was just inches from where the upper tread disappeared into the cowling. Suddenly, his jiggles worked, and the engine roared to life. Sputter, sputter, putt, putt, and without warning the lugs were moving backwards down the hill. It is beyond the dark reaches of my imagination to grasp the horror he experienced as the tread dragged his left boot and then his left leg underneath the cowling. It would have been another minute, perhaps, before the rest of his body followed his leg. The bones would have snapped so that his body could fit beneath the cowling. Mercifully, unconsciousness would have taken away his suffering after the first minute.

Evidently, his body separated at the pelvis. Then gradually, most of what used to be the man went through the cowling, while other bloody pieces fell to the rocks beside the Caterpillar. As the dozer continued its slow downhill descent, parts of the man's body that had gone through the cowling were thrown free from the moving treads. Most of those pieces were run over again by the dozer's front blade, which had been in the down-position. That front blade made a pulp of what remained of this poor man's body as it dragged over everything again. An investigation revealed that the wiring problem had likely caused the engine to die just another 10 yards down the hillside. That is where the owner found it after he went see why the homesteader hadn't made the routine radio call that evening.

This was a simple investigation initiated by the insurer of the Caterpillar's owner. The insurance company's claim representative in the Midwest, had no idea what the reality of life in the archipelago stretching off toward Japan is like. He was concerned that the owner may have been negligent in causing the homesteader's death, highly unlikely, but the possibility still needed to be evaluated. The Alaska State Trooper summoned to the scene the next day picked up as many pieces as he could find and placed them in a plastic body bag. The black bag turned out to be far larger than what was needed to transport the small scattering of remains that he recovered near the creek.

My work showed that the Caterpillar owner had exercised appropriate diligence in cautioning the homesteader about the wiring issues with the engine. No money had changed hands. The loaner was not liable under the simple principle that the homesteader was familiar with the operation of this bulldozer and had assumed the risk of operating it himself.

As a side note, the Troopers didn't ultimately have any luck tracking down relatives of the hermit-homesteader. Even if they could have, it was highly unlikely there would have been a liability settlement. As with the majority of the claims, when my work was finished, I closed my file and dove into the next assignment, never finding out what happened in the following years. Did the Kodiak Island Borough or Lake and Peninsula Borough end up taking over the property and perhaps auctioning it off to another adventurer later, or did it eventually collapse during annual gully-washing storms and finally become an assemblage of miscellaneous timbers sticking up from between the rocks where the mountainside stream had declared victory?

18

Heroin on the Palmer-Wasilla

President Dwight D. Eisenhower initiated the Interstate Highway System in 1956, three years before Alaska became the 49th state. Fifty years later, in a report on the golden anniversary of the Interstate Highway System held in Washington, DC, I heard a National Public Radio commentator say, "Every American city with a population of 50,000 or more is on an Interstate Highway." I think that even my car radio was taken aback by his ignorance. I was driving up Rabbit Creek Road, and I mused, "What interstate connects Alaska's three biggest cities?"

Less than a quarter of the towns in Alaska even have roads reaching beyond their boundaries. Where there are highways, many are gravel, and even those made of asphalt are two lanes. Inside the cities of Juneau, Fairbanks, and Anchorage, there are what might appear to be Lower 48 freeways, but they don't go far. The greatest advantage of Alaska's road system is that small populations and immense distances between towns make for light traffic on most routes, so the frequency of accidents is low, but the severity of the impact is often catastrophic. As rural routes in Alaska have become increasingly crowded—much like what was seen around other American cities 75 years ago—the calls for limited access, divided highways have also increased.

One tragically too-busy two-laner serves as the main link between Palmer and Wasilla in the Matanuska-Susitna Borough (Mat-Su). Once a farming road linking two little towns, the Palmer-Wasilla Highway is now a thoroughfare serving these twin Anchorage bedroom communities. Back when it was built, property was cheap. But by the 21st century, the lure of virgin spruce forests, bucolic dairy farms, and giant-cabbage fields had been tainted by strip malls and a Walmart Supercenter.

One thing that remains a factor on the Palmer-Wasilla Highway is the number of Alaskan lives it takes every year. Even with recent improvements, the carnage hasn't stopped. The Mat-Su today has a hospital complex that includes a heliport and a trauma center, but prior to 2006, ambulances shuttled casualties and survivors to a little hospital in Palmer.

In 2003, a 28-year-old Russian immigrant who turned out to have an amazing capacity for deception, landed a job driving a 16-passenger Mat-Su charity bus for the elderly and disabled. His territory covered 300 square miles of picking up and dropping off clients at clinics and adult daycare centers, many of which were located along the Palmer-Wasilla Highway. Especially during the evening commute, the road had one busy lane in each direction and was almost devoid of left turn lanes or turnouts for the side-streets.

The Russian driver had a pronounced accent but a good command of English. He knew what he was doing from his time as a bus driver in Moscow before he emigrated. What wasn't immediately clear was his dependence on marijuana and alcohol—which the charity didn't test for at the time he was hired—and the most troubling one, heroin.

He befriended a regular passenger, a 20-year-old adult daycare resident who was developmentally disabled, who rode on this Russian's shuttle Monday through Friday every week. The two became occasional heroin partners, shooting up during the driver's early-dinner break.

One late fall afternoon—it was dark but not yet snowy—they headed from Wasilla toward Palmer with six other adult passengers on the bus, none of whom were aware that the driver and one passenger were flying high on heroin. A 45-year-old woman in a Ford Tempo was also traveling toward Palmer, about a quarter mile ahead of the minibus. The woman in the Tempo signaled a left turn and stopped in the roadway to wait for a break in the long line of oncoming commuter headlights on the way to Wasilla. In anticipation of the turn, she had cranked the steering wheel to the left, a sad mistake.

The charity bus was cruising at 55 MPH, a bit over the speed limit. The heroin-injected driver had crested his drug-high right about then, and his neurons were in a state of pacifying rapture. The bus sailed into the back of the Tempo without even braking (there were no skid marks indicating any attempt to stop).

Because the Tempo's front wheels were cocked to the left when it was rear-ended, it was catapulted into the front driver's side of an oncoming Toyota Corolla driven by a mother of two, who was headed home from work, and whose children fortunately weren't in the car. She died instantly of crushing wounds, and her head burst through the driver's side window. The woman in the Tempo sustained cervical and spinal injuries, commonly known as whiplash. She remained conscious and was still moaning in pain when the EMT's arrived. After the collision, the bus ran off the road and into a broad ditch where—miraculously—it stayed on its wheels. Every passenger on the bus was injured, most with minor lacerations and a few with broken bones.

The collision tied up the highway for hours, while generating a massive response from all the nearby fire departments and their medical first-responders, as well as the Alaska State Troopers. Fire department aid cars and commercial ambulances transported the victims to the hospital in Palmer. The woman in the Corolla was pronounced dead at the scene, while the driver of the Tempo was helicoptered from the Palmer hospital to an Anchorage hospital with a more complete trauma center.

The tiny emergency department in Palmer was in chaos. The Russian driver had only sustained minor injuries, so after he was bandaged, he hatched a plan to save his skin. He knew that the Troopers would be coming to interview him as soon as they figured out that he was the minibus driver. So he had a taxi drive him ten miles back along the Palmer-Wasilla to his small, rented house.

Once home, he immediately began gulping down vodka. He also grabbed his stash of marijuana joints and smoked one after another. When he saw the police cruiser enter his driveway, he threw himself onto the couch under a blanket, with the bottle of vodka lying on the floor beside him. When the officer came through the door, the man cried hot tears, telling the officer between sobs that he had been so overcome by grief that he had come home and taken anything he could get a hold of—yes, Sir, even heroin—to dull the pain.

The Trooper took him back to the hospital for a toxicology test. While the results showed that he had alcohol, marijuana and heroin in his bloodstream, they didn't show how long those substances had been there. For his rear-end collision, a probable involuntary manslaughter charge would arise if the substance abuse could be linked to the at-fault crash, and that would mean a prison sentence. But this man had succeeded in hiding the fact that he was flying high on heroin when he crashed into the Tempo.

Months later, I interviewed the man at the charity's headquarters in the tiny Mat-Su village where it was headquartered, in the presence of the charity's attorney. As I questioned the Russian driver, a feeling of overwhelming disgust gripped me. He was nonchalant about the accident, with not even the remotest shred of remorse for what he had done, nor did he utter a single word of grief about the kids that he had made orphans.

I would never have known about the timing of the driver's heroin use if it weren't for the burning conscience of the young passenger who had used heroin with him that day. Feeling guilty, this young man called me and said he needed to talk. So—after I checked with counsel—I made an appointment to meet him. He told me the whole story about how he and the driver had injected heroin just before the fateful drive, something they had done several times before that. In his talk with me, he might have cleared some of his feelings of guilt. He was just a passenger, and he felt responsibility, unlike the driver who felt nothing.

The attorney to whom I was reporting told me that the information I had gathered would not be relevant unless I were subpoenaed to testify in the future. That never happened, and my investigation went into the filing cabinet marked "closed," while various claims departments and attorneys sorted out who should pay how much money and to whom.

As often happened in my line of work, I went on to another investigation without knowing the outcome of settlement litigation, a process that could take anywhere from months to years. Additionally, as my file was archived off-site for the requisite seven years, I was never informed regarding final settlements. To this day, it is hard to drive past the site of the accident without experiencing feelings of disgust and frustration.

19

Hirschbraten

Wood-Tikchik State Park in Southwest Alaska covers 1.6 million acres. Alaska's state parks are huge by any reckoning, but its national parks are even bigger. Denali National Park covers 6 million acres, and Wrangell-St. Elias National Park is 13.6 million acres. By comparison, the nation of Switzerland is 10.2 million acres. In the Lower 48, there are some incredibly large state park treasures, too. New York's Adirondack State Park, covering a fifth of the state, is as big as Denali. However, most parks and preserves below the 49th parallel are smaller (e.g., Mount Rainier National Park, at 236,581 acres).

There are no roads inside Wood-Tikchik State Park, and the Aleknagik Ranger Station near Dillingham is its single administrative facility. Paradoxically, there are some private in-holdings, parcels of land that were homesteaded in the 19th century. Some parcels have been snatched up by agents of billionaires, celebrities, and American televangelists to build fly-in hunting and fishing lodges on, complete with diesel-generated electricity, running water, and septic. The opulence of these select lodges is in line with their owners' yachts and Riviera winter homes, but out of place in the absolute wilderness and amid the remote Yup'ik villages of the region.

A step down from those palaces are the fishing lodges on the islands of the Tongass National Forest archipelago in the Alaska panhandle, Kodiak and into the Aleutians, as well as up in the grand interior lying to the north of Denali.

One of those establishments was Ekwok Lodge, run by a congenial and industrious couple from Bavaria. They grew to love Southwest Alaska and decided they would connect well-heeled folks from Germany, Switzerland, and Austria with the world-class chinook, or king, salmon fishing the region was famous for. The lodge was located a couple miles downriver from the Yup'ik Eskimo village that shares its name. I don't know how many highly successful years Ekwok Lodge had before it was forced to close

194

in 2008. It wasn't the economic recession at the time that led to its closure, but rather health issues—namely cancer—faced by the operators.

The Bavarian couple that ran Ekwok Lodge spent their winters holding multimedia presentations for prospective guests across Germany, where they offered samples of Nushagak River kippers and soft-smoked salmon. The lodge consisted of a main building with a dining area and a social room with broad windows looking out over the river below, and an almost constantly crackling fire in a huge river-rock fireplace. Outbuildings held hotel-style apartments and dorms, with staff coming from Germany on temporary summer work permits.

Ekwok Lodge was a German angler's dream—for whom the mere thought of landing giant Nushagak River kings could be enough to empty their savings accounts. Most guests flew into Anchorage from Frankfurt, then on to Dillingham, and finally by boat two hours upriver to the lodge. Any stragglers would have the option of taking one of the single-engine mail and freight planes flying daily from Dillingham to the villages of Portage Creek, Ekwok, Koliganek, and New Stuyahok. By pre-arrangement, the lodge's skipper would look for the plane on approach to the gravel landing strip and head out in a skiff a couple miles upriver to meet the guest at the Ekwok Village dock.

Despite the obvious poverty in the nearby village, Ekwok Lodge offered no maintenance jobs, no apprenticeships, no dining room jobs, nothing to the Natives who were neighbors. The intent was not to integrate into Alaska. Rather, Ekwok Lodge was designed to mimic in class and comfort the Bavarian hunting lodges of the nineteenth century.

The cuisine included Sauerbraten, Schweinekotelete (pork cutlets), and Hirschbraten (venison imported from Germany). But there was one grand locally sourced menu item: Nushagak River king salmon, often served as cold-smoked Räucherlachs (what an American deli would call *lox*). In the evening, a five-course dinner was followed by digestifs and Schnapps by the fireplace, then later still by Abendbrot (dark bread, sausages, cheese, and fresh berries) before bedtime. Three miles away in the village of Ekwok, population 110, the traditional Natives' diet was moose, bear, dried salmon, berries, and seeds; but lodge guests likely knew nothing of that.

At the edge of the compound, facing in the direction of the village, sat the lodge's most critically important structure of all, a steel-frame maintenance shop housing an industrial diesel power plant and a smaller emergency generator. The building was also home to the lodge's central hot water heaters and well pump controls. Outside, above ground, were a giant diesel fuel tank, a large propane tank, and a smaller gasoline tank to fuel the outboard motors on the guest boats, and for the lodge's four-wheeler. All the fuel had to come upriver by barge from the Port of Dillingham.

One late afternoon in July, the lodge guests brought their catch of kings up from the river, and as was the practice, they deposited them in the guest refrigerators to be later frozen or turned into Räucherlachs. While small salmon were around fifteen pounds, many kings were as big as fifty.

The before-dinner libations of American whiskey or European cognac were self-serve in the fireplace room. Upon a bell being rung, the guests proceeded into the white tablecloth dining room. That evening, thick clouds came over the river and the light began to grow dim. Around 10 PM, the lights flickered, came back to life for a minute, flickered a couple more times, and then went dark. The emergency generator kicked into gear to power the crucial refrigerators and provide the lodge with minimal lighting.

The alarm about the situation spread quickly among the guests, and all the men left the fireplace room and headed for the maintenance building.

One otherwise minor detail that would end up being crucial in the events that followed was the fact, as one might expect from organized Germans, that the maintenance shop was thoroughly stocked with a wide assortment of tools and high-quality equipment. Above everything in the shop, an array of bright fluorescent lights hung from the ceiling, and these were connected to both the main generator and the back-up power plant. Thus, one could easily work through the night inside this structure.

The reason that the male guests had jumped into action was that they were all members of an affinity group of engineers—mechanical, industrial, civil, electrical, and chemical. They had been tinkerers in their youths, building science projects, winning awards, working on cars, repairing engines—all just for fun. But now some were faculty members of universities and trade schools. If given the choice, they might not have elected to spend their vacation in an establishment so out of sync with the local Native culture, but being able to relax and speak German rather than laboring with English had perhaps been a selling point.

That night, there would be no Abendbrot or fireside nightcap for the engineers. They gathered in a convocation, elected a team leader and charged into battle. They quickly discovered that the power plant failure was the result of sabotage. Sulfuric acid and sand, lots of it, were found in the engine oil and diesel fuel. The mixture was also found in a handful of other less-important openings in the equipment, an indicator that the perpetrator(s) probably didn't know much about how the power plant functioned. The group of engineers deduced that the foreign substances had been present from a couple days to a week prior to the outage. They also marveled at the design characteristics that had allowed the enormous American generator to chug along for so long under the conditions.

The engineers conjured up an improbable workaround to coax the power plant back to life, albeit less efficiently and with some exhaust smoke. Thanks to their high-level teamwork, before the chef and kitchen helpers had even gotten out of bed in the morning, the main generator was once again up and running. Except for the engineers leaving their respective partners alone at the breakfast table that morning to slip back into bed for a well-earned nap, it was the beginning of another normal day of fishing on the Nushagak.

The verdict was that the damage was fatal, but that the power plant would probably make it through to the September end of the season if the lodge's luck held. The repair or replacement would have to be addressed in the factory, an enormous logistical problem, made all the more urgent by the fact that river barge traffic would cease at freeze-up, usually before Halloween.

When the generator went down, the lodge manager immediately reported the situation to its Anchorage-based insurer. The claims manager there was a woman who today remains a best friend of mine, Clare

Hiratsuka. The loss of the generator and potential income created an untenable exposure for this small insurance company, meaning that they needed to immediately report the details of the claim for damages to their re-insurance company. (Insurance companies need insurance, too, for when they are hit with losses that their actuaries didn't forecast. There are roughly 20 such well-capitalized reinsurance companies in the world, mostly in financial centers such as New York City, Zürich, or London, but some are headquartered in tax havens such as Bermuda.)

The day after being assigned the case, I embarked on the necessary air and boat journey to reach Ekwok Lodge. One positive bit of serendipity was that—unknown to the company—my fluency in German would become crucial in assembling the facts of the case.

The weather forecast for Dillingham was heavy rain, low cloud cover, and occasional gusty wind—typical for that time of year. In the office, I asked my most trusted coworker Joyce to cover for me for the following couple days. The Alaska Airlines jet could land in Dillingham, but the second leg of the trip to Ekwok Village in a six-seater wasn't a sure thing. In Dillingham, I made my way along the mud-puddled main drag to a building housing the agents for two bush air services that flew upriver, as well as to villages in the opposite direction such as Quinhagak on the Kanektok River.

I was standing at the main air service counter at noon, where I asked the nice lady in her floral pattern kuspuk, a typical Yup'ik anorak, to check me in for the flight to Ekwok. She said she was sorry, but that the entire Nushagak River drainage was on a weather hold. She offered me coffee and told me to make myself comfortable on one of two cracked-vinyl couches. Six other people huddled in the ramshackle office waiting for the cloud ceiling to lift.

The monotony was suddenly interrupted by an entertaining spectacle when a white, twin-engine corporate jet came screaming in for a landing. It bore no insignias other than the requisite fuselage numbers, and judging by its approach through the low ceiling it probably had advanced avionics on board, just like the big airliners. At first, it taxied over to the far side of the runway, where I hadn't even noticed an amphibious float plane, a single-engine Cessna up high on its wheels, waiting. In the distance, four figures descended from the jet and immediately climbed the ladder into the Cessna. A pilot from the Cessna loaded up their baggage, and then it took off.

For the next part of the show, the palatial jet taxied over to our side of the airport and stopped in front of the bush-air office. The pilot and copilot, clad in ties and crisp uniforms that looked bizarre in rural Alaska, walked in and up to the lady at the counter. I had been chatting with her, and so happened to be standing at the counter when the fellows interrupted. The pilot pulled out an American Express card and purchased thousands of dollars' worth of jet fuel. He explained that they had flown nonstop from St. Louis. I was unaware that small jets like that had such a long-range capability. They asked where they could park it, preferably somewhere they could have regular access for possibly the following two weeks. I asked, "So I assume your passengers flew into a lodge on a lake in Wood-Tikchik, right?" They froze, looked at each other, then exclaimed, "We don't disclose such information." I said, "Okay," and pretended as if nothing had happened.

The pilot then asked the lady where the car rental agency was, and where the Triple-A office might be so that they could grab a road map. She stared blankly in response, so they asked the same question of me, also asking if I could recommend a decent hotel close to the airport.

I first began, "Do you know where you are? You're in Dillingham, Alaska, and there is no Triple-A. The one gas station might have a road map, but I doubt it. There are several miles of roads in town, one of which is asphalted and runs for 25 miles out to the community of Aleknagik. That's it. As for a hotel, I know of two: one is near a cafe and the other is a bit closer to the airport." Because I came to Dillingham on claims work occasionally, I knew where to rent a car. If push comes to shove, you can usually find something at the junk yard. They huffed and walked back out to their jet. I went back to my couch and entertained myself with the thoughts of what these two urbanites would possibly do to entertain themselves in Dillingham for two weeks.

Two hours later, the kuspuk lady told those waiting to head up the Nushagak that another pilot had reported that the weather was improving. "Improving" in this situation simply meant that the ground fog had lifted enough that a plane could follow the river while flying just below the clouds.

A Yup'ik woman and a man were waiting to fly further upriver to New Stuyahok, and the kuspuk woman told us we would board as soon as our pilot finished loading the freight. The young man came to the door and called out, "One passenger for Ekwok and two for New Stuyahok, follow me." Because I have long legs, the pilot put me up front next to him. When he loaded the other two into the back, the plane tipped backwards onto its tail. Unfazed, the pilot proceeded to open the cargo door and unload about half of the boxes. He remarked, "Well, they'll just have to wait until tomorrow or the day after that."

With the aircraft now properly balanced, we took off in the direction of the nearby Nushagak delta. Then we turned upriver. We were so close to the low-hanging clouds just above the river that I mused to myself that the plane's tail was probably putting scratch marks in the clouds. The altimeter on the dash showed that we were under 200 vertical feet above the river. It was close enough that I could even make out the eyes and ears of the caribou below.

The pilot landed smoothly on the gravel runway in Ekwok, and as instructed, I made my way from the airstrip down to the dock with its hanging salmon nets and a collection of skiffs, one of which was Ekwok Lodge's own boat, which the skipper had brought to Ekwok village to pick me up.

When I arrived the lights were on, leaving me befuddled—wasn't the generator destroyed? Also, most of the guests were still out fishing up and down the river as usual. A few skiffs were already returning to the lodge's dock, loaded with bounties of enormous kings. They shouted greetings to me in German, and I answered back. I wondered what emergency I had even come to investigate.

Much of my work was already done, given that the German engineers had written up a detailed report for me to reference. My only task would be to translate everything into English back at the office. At the lodge, it only took about three hours to capture the requisite photos and measurements and prepare my preliminary field report. Forgoing a Löwenbräu to do some paperwork was my only hardship. The dinner that night was Hischbraten mit Kartoffelklöse along with Gemischtes Salat, Rotkohl, und Sahnentorte for dessert. Afterwards, I chatted with the guests over Schnapps and Kleingebäck. Even the magazines on the coffee tables were in German. It was as if I were in Germany making new friends. Occasionally, I glanced out the window and snapped back to reality—I was not looking at the Allgäu mountains, but at the black-spruce forests lining the shores of Alaska's Nushagak River.

I retired to my room and slept until breakfast. I was due to fly out that afternoon when the mail plane arrived at Ekwok Village. However, as I had suspected, there would be no flying that day. By that point, I was no stranger to getting weathered in, and to the need to sometimes get creative finding a place to spend the night. In Kotlik, for example, the kindly proprietor of the village store had allowed me to haul out one of the plastic wrapped mattresses from the hardware section to the widest aisle in the store, between the potato chips and the Cap'n Crunch. In Upper Kalskag, I bargained with the town clerk for permission to sleep in their drunk tank, which I hoped would stay empty throughout the night. Fortunately, the kindly woman ended up finding me a place in a Conex unit that had been fashioned into an apartment for workers in the Village Safe Water Program.

In stark contrast, here at Ekwok Lodge I was faced with the prospect of having no other option but to consume round after round of gourmet cuisine accompanied by Pilsener beer and Rhine wine, followed by dark coffee and perhaps a slice of Schwarzwälder Kirschtorte. And for breakfast and a late snack, there was always Nushagak River Räucherlachs. I began to hope I'd be stuck there for a week.

On day two, I tried to call the Ekwok Village VPSO, or "Village Public Safety Officer," but he was on leave and wasn't expected to return for another week. When I did reach him two weeks later by phone from Anchorage, he had no interest in opening an investigation into the allegation of sabotage.

The third day at Ekwok Lodge dawned sunny and calm. I called the air service in Dillingham using the lodge's radio-phone, and they arranged an afternoon pickup. After being motored upriver to the village of Ekwok, I bid the skipper Auf Wiedersehen! Vielen herzlichen Dank! (Goodbye! Many heartfelt thanks!)

I disembarked and walked through the village and up the hill to the airstrip. After an hour, I saw my plane on its approach. My timing had been good by rural Alaska standards, where hours long waits are the norm. The local joke for people like me who flew in small planes a lot went, "If you've got time to spare, go by air."

Hirschbraten

Back in Dillingham, I had 10 minutes to dash over to the Alaska Airlines building and snag a seat on the jet to Anchorage. I'd be home in time for dinner. Disappointingly, it would be microwaved Lean Cuisine, not Hirschbraten.

20

Mouse in the Potato Chips

There are two Costcos in Anchorage, while Fairbanks and Juneau each have one, as well. In several towns connected to those cities by roads or boat, enterprising locals have started unaffiliated businesses re-selling groceries from Costco. They travel hundreds of miles to load up a trailer with popular items and come home to sell them with a small markup.

In 1996 I received an assignment from an Atlanta-based insurance company, and along with it came a letter of representation from a Valdez attorney. He asserted that his clients had suffered because they bought a giant bag of Nalley Potato Chips from the local Costco reseller. (Costco itself had nothing to do with the matter.) When his clients reached into the bag, they pulled out a fried and salted mouse. Not only were these innocent victims traumatized by touching the odious thing, but they were worried about the diseases that Nalley had potentially exposed them to.

My first thought was, Heavens! This is rural Alaska. Any other person would have just fed the dead mouse to the dog and enjoyed the rest of the chips. Naturally, in my first telephone call to the attorney I was more circumspect. I allowed that this attorney's clients might have suffered as he claimed.

This lawyer hadn't yet named a dollar figure in a settlement demand. It looked to me like he was trying to see if Nalley would offer him cash to keep the matter from making the news. He probably was counting on the fact that Valdez had a unit of the Alaska Court System. If he filed suit—even if it were deemed to be frivolous in the end—it would cost serious money to hire an Anchorage defense attorney to take the case in Valdez. (Valdez, located on Prince William Sound, is a 5-1/2-hour, scenic mountain drive or a 50-minute flight from Anchorage.)

As it turned out, the insurance company and its client, the potato chip maker, decided to resist. The lawyer told me that the fried mouse was preserved in a box inside his office refrigerator. He would allow me to view it and take photographs—but not touch or probe—when I came to Valdez. The insurance company wanted me to meet and interview his clients, too, as well as get pictures of the residence and the exact place where the potato chip mouse had been found. The lawyer agreed to the conditions.

So one day in his office, I sat down to hear the tearful story first-hand from the middle-aged husband and wife, who apparently dined quite often on oversized bags of potato chips. They were five days into eating from this bag, which they closed after every use with a spring-loaded chip-saver, when they came upon the fried mouse. The shock and revulsion made them both want to vomit. They said they feared they might be coming down with a disease from touching the vermin, but that they hadn't been to the doctor…yet.

After the clients left the office, their lawyer brought out the evidence. It was a skinny little critter, and it did, indeed, look like it had been fried. But at the same time, it stunk. I pondered, Why would a piece of animal flesh that had been industrially fried and salted emit an odor? When the attorney took me to the plaintiffs' rusted, single-wide mobile home near the Valdez Airport, I saw where the clients had lain the Nalley bag on the floor next to their La-Z-Boy, in front their mondo-screen TV.

Nalley, a traditional mainstay of Pacific Northwest pickles, canned chili, and potato chips was at one time located in the "Nalley Valley" district of Tacoma, Washington. Before the company was subsumed under a mega food enterprise, it had faced various complaints over its sanitary procedures. This fact made a fried mouse in a potato chip bag seem a bit more plausible.

By the time the big Nalley bag ended up in Valdez, however, the company was on a different path. All potato chips were made at a multi-brand factory in Salt Lake City, Utah, where regardless of packaging, many different brand names were exactly the same product. Because Nalley products had figured prominently in the cupboards of generations of Pacific Northwesterners, the corporation marketed their mass-produced potato chips headed for the Pacific Northwest under the Nalley brand to capitalize on customer loyalty.

While the attorney insisted that the life form inside the bag was indeed a mouse, I wasn't so sure. I wanted it to be taxonomically identified, and I explained my suspicion about the specimen to the insurance company, which could render the attorney's claim invalid. I wondered if maybe the bag of chips had simply been lying open on the floor, and if a local rodent had climbed in for its own snacking pleasure. When the bag was clipped shut again, the critter would have fallen to the bottom, where because of the salt, it would first die of thirst. Its body would then become desiccated and its surface skin saturated with vegetable oil.

The insurance company told me to proceed with the identification. For background, in 1993, there was an outbreak of the Hanta virus among the deer mouse population in the "four corners" states of the American Southwest. The disease was taken seriously because it could ultimately infect humans, and the fear of transmission had spurred federal funding to research wild populations of small rodents, what most people referred to as "field mice." At the time of the potato chip mouse investigation, two American universities had research projects in motion examining small rodents. One of these just happened to be the University of Alaska Fairbanks (UAF).

When I met the Valdez lawyer at the Anchorage airport, he had the dead "mouse" in a Styrofoam container. I cornily quipped that this was his "carrion luggage." He eked out an uneasy chuckle and we boarded the 40-minute flight to Fairbanks.

The rodent research project was housed in the underground level of the immense UAF Museum, a place with rooms upon rooms of trays upon trays holding samples. In the main area, about 20 staff and volunteer biologists were working to identify various dead, mouse-like creatures from all over North America. Despite large ventilation fans, the stench hit our noses almost immediately after we walked in. But that was nothing compared to the odor coming from a hundred yards away, where a special enclosure held dead rodents splayed out for maggots to dine upon. After a couple days, the result was skeletons that researchers could then mount, label, and place in archival trays.

The young professor who headed the rodent taxonomy program had agreed to provide us with a certified identification of our rodent in exchange for a small contribution to the program. Furthermore, he wanted to retain the specimen until all the work was completed; and he verified in writing that it would not be touched or modified in any way. After a few days, both the attorney in Valdez and I received the document. The critter we had brought him was a desiccated "dusky shrew." This rodent was common in the Chugach Mountains where Valdez is situated, but by bizarre coincidence also in the Wasatch Mountains, where Salt Lake City is located. Thus, while we now knew the species of the "mouse," we were no closer to finding out where the little guy was actually from.

The director of the UAF program suggested that the next logical step was a DNA analysis, but that would mean cutting away a small tissue sample. The attorney agreed. A few days later, I got a call. The director said they had evidently not been careful enough in sampling the dusky shrew's flesh, as the DNA analysis came back revealing more about the makeup of vegetable oil than about the shrew. They cut out a deeper sample and tried again.

This time, the analysis was valid. The DNA profile showed the dusky shrew was 82 times more similar to those found in Alaska's Chugach Mountains than to those scurrying around Salt Lake City. The UAF professor told me he would follow up the call with a written, sworn statement. I thought to myself, If that dusky shrew had managed to get into a potato chip bag in Utah, it would have needed to take a long airplane ride from Alaska to get there.

I called the insurance company and then the attorney to tell them the news. He said that he'd notify his clients and send written confirmation of his withdrawal from the case. He noted that he would not be flying up to Fairbanks to pick up the carrion.

In the end, our dusky shrew that had the extraordinary honor of flying between a lawyer and an adjuster in the passenger compartment of an Alaska Airlines jet, would end up in UAF's research archives. Even if they could, I doubted the hungry maggots the shrew was fed to would have complained about the added salt and cooking oil.

21

Like a Dropped Watermelon

When the rain in Ketchikan is blowing sideways, most cruise-ship passengers select a bus excursion, rather than venturing out on the streets in the tacky plastic rain ponchos they are issued. However, the passengers from Western Oregon, Washington, and British Columbia are the exceptions; they bring rain parkas, rain pants, and even GORE-TEX walking shoes.

Topping the list of weather-protected excursions to tantalize the largest possible number of cruisers is Ketchikan's fleet of Duck Boats. These military amphibious landing craft have been converted into Plexiglas-enclosed, heated, pleasure craft, and they are huge. Prior to the events in this story, the Duck Boats regularly drove directly up to the cruise ship boarding ramps so that passengers could avoid the wind and rain.

As usual, one hyper-drizzly day in the middle of summer, the first half of the narrated Duck Boat tour took place on the streets of Ketchikan and around its lowland forest parkland. The high point of the trip was when the amphibious boats returned downtown to the overlook at the small boat harbor, providing a view of the eclectic mix of fishing boats docked there in between commercial openings.

It was there that the driver of this one of the ducks donned his skipper's cap, guiding the amphibian down a concrete ramp and into the water alongside trollers, seiners, and gillnetters. With the Duck Boat rocking gently on the water, the skipper switched the engine power to the propellers, and they motored off. Passing beyond the jetty that protected the little harbor, the Duck Boat revved up for a trip up and down the Tongass Narrows. It cruised by the Alaska Marine Highway terminal, passed cargo ships and cruise ships, and maneuvered around the shuttle ferry to the airport.

At the end of the saltwater leg of the trip, the Duck Boat returned to the small boat harbor, and the skipper did the reverse procedure. After nosing the craft in past the fishing fleet, with a final push from the propellers the Duck Boat's wheels contacted the concrete, and in a quick changeover act, the skipper became driver once again. The diesel engine roared, and the Duck Boat emerged out of the water like a breaching whale. Unless it was raining extremely hard—as it was on this day—the Duck Boat would pause in the parking lot so an attendant could hose off the saltwater.

The tour was almost over, and it was a straight shot back to the ship. The huge conveyance turned the corner and headed south to Front Street and then directly out onto the cruise ship dock itself. The passengers began stowing their cameras and lunch sacks in their backpacks. They wouldn't be exposed to the elements but briefly, as the driver would try to get the Duck Boat's exit stairs as close as possible to the ship's boarding area.

In the meantime, on the corner of Front Street that abuts the cruise ship dock, a petite Illinois woman had been shopping. She braved the elements in her yellow, plastic poncho to drop into a souvenir shop, and as a shopkeeper later related, to get gifts for her grandchildren. After coming out the door of the first store, she headed in the direction of another shop on the opposite side of Front Street. In her right hand she held a plastic bag containing a couple kids' T-shirts and a plush toy moose, while with her left she tried to keep the wind-tortured poncho out of her face. The Duck Boat was moving so slowly now that the engine was nearly silent; and with the wind and rain, the Illinois lady couldn't have heard it approaching.

For the driver, the ship's boarding area was just 60 yards ahead and to the right. Sitting up high and peering over the bow, he had a grand view of the dock, but the prow made it impossible to see what was directly below and in front. (As far as I know, the Duck Boats were later fitted with outboard mirrors and remote cameras.) The woman stepped into the street. The driver felt something akin to a tiny speed-bump, and a wave of horror rolled over him; he knew the pavement there was smooth. "Oh, my God, No! No! No!" He braked and, while ordering the passengers to stay seated, extended the ladder so that he could descend to the pavement.

The preceding details come from eyewitness interviews, but what follows is based on video recorded at the scene. The Ketchikan Visitors Bureau at 131 Front Street had an exterior surveillance camera mounted on the outside of its second floor. By a fluke, at that moment it was aimed at the place where this woman was beginning to walk across the street.

First the prow of the Duck Boat hit her in the head, and then she dropped to the pavement, where the right front wheel rolled over her skull. It popped like a watermelon dropped off the back of a produce truck. What had been a human being's essence was now a morass of skull fragments, brain matter, and blood.

In short order, the EMT's arrived—the fire station was nearby. The ship sent crew members with blankets to form a wall around the grisly scene and ensure passengers descending from the Duck Boat or down the loading ramp from the ship wouldn't see what had happened. The Ketchikan Police were also on the scene. There were a couple passersby who saw what had occurred, but none of those aboard the Duck Boat knew anything for sure, except that the driver had told them not to get out of their seats after shrieking in horror and stopping the craft.

Death claims are straightforward from an adjuster's point of view. There are no bills for medical treatment, and there are obviously no interviews with the deceased. After submitting my report to the attorney representing the Duck Boat's insurer, including recorded interview summaries, my job was done. However, the wrangling among multiple law offices had just begun. The City of Ketchikan was on the firing line for allegations of poor dock design. The cruise ship supposedly bore responsibility, too, because it sold the tour on board despite the protection of its lawyer-crafted, essentially bomb-proof hold-harmless language in the fine print on the tickets. The driver did the job the way he always had, but still the other attorneys tried to put the lion's share of the blame on him. Fortunately, the Duck Boat company had high liability limits on its insurance policy, and that would mean that its continued existence as a company would not be endangered by probable huge payments to settle the claim in the future.

From Ketchikan, I took the evening flight back to Anchorage. After stops in Sitka and Juneau, Alaska Airlines served dinner. A public health nurse was next to me, and we exchanged small talk about how the meal was actually pretty good for airplane food. My investigation was, as always, proprietary, so I didn't tell her why I had been in Ketchikan. Coincidentally, we started talking about the rapid disconnect of senses when an accident destroys one's brain. I thought of the Illinois lady. She might have been thinking about how much her grandkids would like their new plush toy moose when for her the lights suddenly went out.

22

Not All Angels Have Wings

Since its launch in 1915, Seward's Mount Marathon Race on the Fourth of July has grown ever more popular. Today, it draws many thousands in a state where there aren't very many thousands. Running magazines bill it as "the roughest 5K race on the planet." Typically starting with the juniors at 9 AM, the women at 11 AM, and the men at 2 PM, mountain runners depart the starting line at Fourth and Adams in front of First National Bank Alaska. At that point, the course is roughly 30 feet above sea level; they run, clamber, crawl, and climb to the 3,022 ft. summit and then immediately turn around to descend—some of them appearing to be falling and others actually doing so. The fittest of the fit can manage the 3.1-mile round trip in under 45 minutes.

Race fans and the party-minded alike line the route out of town and up on to the lower reaches of the mountain. For many of the onlookers, the drinking part of the Mount Marathon celebration begins in the days leading up to the event. This is when Providence Seward Medical Center's emergency department does triple-time with revelers that tumble off their four-wheelers, fall into campfires, blow their fingers off with firecrackers, nearly drown, or actually drown in the Resurrection River. They also get loads of people with all sorts of gastrointestinal distress, resulting from oversights like leaving the potato salad out overnight. But far worse than all of this are the traffic accidents on the Seward Highway.

Following decades of campaigns against drunk driving on New Year's Eve, most everyone knows you should stay home, stay overnight, or take a taxi on that holiday. But the Fourth of July is exponentially bloodier. While New Year's crashes mostly aren't high speed and usually occur within a 10- to 20-minute drive from urban hospitals, Fourth of July accidents are the opposite. Campsites are generally located up twisting two-lane mountain or seashore roads. And people often don't wait until they're safely at camp to pop open a cold one.

Seward is three hours by highway from Anchorage—most of it just two lanes. This is one of the most scenic roadways in Alaska, making it popular with tourists and wintertime backcountry skiers and snowmachiners. But it is also a primary commercial artery. First it goes along the tidewater to Girdwood and Mount Alyeska and then to the cutoff for Whittier. It turns back the other direction and finally ascends steeply into the mountains of the Kenai Peninsula. The highway climbs from saltwater up to Turnagain Pass at Milepost 70. There are two lanes going up, but coming back down there is only one.

In summer, this section of the Seward Highway below Turnagain Pass is one of the rainiest areas on the Kenai Peninsula. Windshield wipers get a big workout both from what falls from the sky and what sprays from oncoming cars and trucks. In some years, the Mount Marathon races end in the middle of the holiday weekend, giving traffic returning to Anchorage and the Mat-Su a chance to spread out over more than one day. This year was not one of them, and traffic was dense.

A cold rain was falling by the bucketful, and traffic was filling the single descending lane, inspiring impatient drivers to swing out over the double-yellow line to pass. In addition, the road was so soaked with rainwater that rivulets ran downhill on the asphalt.

A married couple in their twenties was returning to Anchorage and the fellow driving was trying to go slow enough to keep his car from hydroplaning in the single downhill lane. In a tsunami of spray, a Camaro carrying four impatient teenagers whooshed by to pass, speeding downhill in the uphill lane, further obscuring visibility for those driving normally downhill.

Both the man and his wife were startled, and she shrieked, "Honey, they're going to die." He said, "Calm down, they'll be okay." She was shaking as she repeated, "No, they're going to die!" As quickly as the Camaro had come upon them, it disappeared into the stormy gloom.

Meanwhile, in the opposite direction, a mom was driving her 5-year-old daughter home to Soldotna in the family's Winnebago. They had been camping in the Mat-Su for the holiday weekend. Dad hadn't been able to join because he had been scheduled to work up on the oil rigs on the North Slope. Traveling about 25 MPH, the Winnebago lumbered uphill against the deluge of rain. Then in an instant—between swipes of the windshield wipers—Mom saw taillights and then headlights appear in the downpour in front of her. She was already in the right-hand lane, but she let off the gas and attempted to steer even closer to the rock embankment.

It was to no avail. The hydroplaning and swerving Camaro hit the Winnebago head-on. The Camaro nose-dived low into the engine compartment of the motorhome, meaning the driver had likely slammed on the brakes at the last moment. Mom and daughter were seated higher, so the force of the impact passed mostly below them. However, this was not the case for Mom's feet. There was an instant of searing pain as both ankles were fractured, while at nearly the same moment a wall of flames—a hellish scene—erupted in front of them where seconds ago the Camaro had been. The intact windshield protected them from the fire and smoke for the time being.

The girl screamed, "Mommy, Mommy!" And the first words out of Mom's mouth were, "You get on the phone to Jesus right now." So this little girl, who fortunately had been uninjured, unbuckled her seat belt, slipped onto the carpet and knelt beside her seat. She bowed her head and asked Jesus for help.

The other couple saw the nearby ball of flames. They stopped and jumped out and were first on the scene. Within seconds, they saw that the entire Camaro was engulfed in flames. The young woman started to utter her own prayers, laced with her anguish. Neither of them could approach the searing heat of the Camaro; they walked a few steps farther toward the motorhome, which was now also on fire.

Through her tears, the young woman made out the figure of the mom behind the Winnebago's steering wheel. Flames and smoke from underneath the chassis began to obscure the length of the motorhome. Then, as she later explained to me in her recorded interview, something incredible happened. The inferno and smoke on the left side of the motorhome paused, and she saw in the sheet-metal siding an opening big enough for her to easily enter. Without a moment's thought for her own safety, she rushed in and grabbed the mother and pulled her out to the wet pavement, ordering the girl to follow. She and her husband then dragged her as carefully as they could farther down, about a car-length beyond the motorhome's rear bumper. Soon, other passersby descended on the scene with tarps and coats and parkas. After a couple minutes, the Winnebago's two propane tanks, located on the right side of the vehicle facing the cliff, exploded. The fiery wreck flipped violently onto its left side, where the group had been minutes earlier.

The emergency medical team and fire engines came from Girdwood, 20 minutes away. All four of the teenagers riding in the Camaro perished. The vehicle was so decimated by the collision and fire that by the time they extinguished it, only four charred corpses were visible. On the police report, the officer said that no toxicology test was administered because it was infeasible, but the report also said that alcohol and/

or drugs had apparently led to the high speed, out-of-control hydroplaning.

The Winnebago's medical payments coverage would take care of the mom's injuries. The Camaro was uninsured, and the motorhome's uninsured motorist property damage and bodily injury liability (UM-PD and UM-BI) coverages kicked in to handle everything else. I never learned anything more about the four kids. There certainly must have been grieving parents, but in my job, I rarely found out about such things.

A few days after the tragedy, the young couple came to my office to provide their witness statements. Often when people have seen a fatality up close, they suffer emotional trauma. However, these two seemed to have come through it all okay. In their stories, they merely explained that they were doing what they needed to do. We finished, and I thanked them while walking them to the elevator. As the doors closed behind them, I said to myself, "Apparently, not all angels have wings."

23

Blood on Ptarmigan Peak

In Chapter 4, I told of my first real encounter with blood in a mountaineering accident, at age 14. Fast-forwarding to 1997 and coinciding with my 50th birthday, I found myself dealing with a great deal more blood spilled by young mountain climbers. In a single accident, 14 climbers had either bled profusely or perished. Two of the group were instructors, while the other twelve were enrolled as students in AWS 105, *Alaska Wilderness Studies Basic Mountaineering,* an offering of the PE department at the University of Alaska Anchorage (UAA). The university's campus affords stunning views of the Chugach Mountains' front range, a few miles away at the edge of the city.

Anchorage is defined by the saltwater of Knik Arm and Turnagain Arm to the southeast and west. On the other side of the city, it is fenced in by the Chugach Mountains. The peaks closest to the city are midgets compared to the rest of the range, but they are impressive because they push up from near sea level. Ptarmigan Peak (4,950 ft.) is 16 miles from downtown, and it is an alpine gem. Chugach National Forest, which comprises seven million acres, is bigger than the state of New Hampshire. Here, there are glaciers with more area than Lower 48 cities, and peaks that reach 13,000 ft.

In 1970, the citizens of Anchorage petitioned the federal government to carve Chugach State Park out of the Chugach National Forest, hoping to create Anchorage's very own backcountry playground. Their work was rewarded with the christening of the 495,000-acre Chugach State Park.

Just after the longest day of the year in 1997, a major tragedy struck the park. The catastrophe decimated the mountaineering program at UAA. But before I tell you about that, I want to talk about a birthday party. Mine.

Blood on Ptarmigan Peak

According to predictions at Seattle's Virginia Mason Hospital, I was supposed to be born on the Fourth of July. But the Ob-Gyn had different plans. He wanted a three-day weekend, so he induced labor on the evening of the Third.

As a kid, a July 3rd birthday meant never having a party on the actual day of my birth, as everyone was always en route to somewhere else for the holiday. Fine by me, though; birthday cake and presents along with firecrackers, hot dogs, home-fried chicken from the farm, and sour-cherry pie. And all of that was combined with scampering around on the pillow basalt at Washington's Deschutes River Falls, blowing up Douglas fir bark boats in the water with firecrackers, and swimming in deep pools so clear you could see the mountain trout 15 feet below your toes. What more could a kid possibly want? Even so, my mother felt guilty year after year because I never got a party on the day of my birthday. Moms are funny that way, I guess.

But on my 50th birthday, Mom decided to fix things once and for all. In March of that year, she sent out written invitations to all my relatives. Well, not invitations really, but orders. There is going to be a July Third birthday party for Kristian, who will fly down from Alaska for the party. Plan ahead! Be there! No exceptions! No excuses! July 3, 1997, 2 PM, at the Erickson condominium at Panorama City in Lacey, Washington.

On June 28, 1997, 12 students enrolled in AWS 105 started out with their two instructors from the Glen Alps Trailhead. They were on a hike to where they would set up a base camp at the foot of Ptarmigan Peak—a practice exercise, given that the peak was so close to the parking lot that climbers could do the whole mountain in a single day. Their colorful tents sat in a meadow below the giant north couloir, something like a snow-filled elevator shaft twisting all the way to the summit ridge.

Early on Sunday, June 29th, the party of 14 ate breakfast and headed out, roped up, with their ice axes and ice-climbing tools in hand. Most carried one of two types of aluminum snow anchors, pickets or flukes. There were four climbing ropes total, and the 12 students and two instructors were distributed in teams of four and three according to their climbing strength. With only two instructors present, some of the rope teams lacked an experienced climber altogether. One of the critical skills discussed earlier in the book that is reinforced through real experience is self-arrest: a technique where when you fall on snow or ice, you first stop yourself from tumbling and then orient your body so the pick of the axe can be dug into the mountain's snow slope, with the slightly less lethal adze adjacent to one's neck. The idea is to stop yourself, get back on your feet, straighten out your gear, adjust your self-esteem, and resume the climb. Those assembled on Ptarmigan Peak that day had all practiced the self-arrest technique on slopes less steep.

The ascent on that warm and sunny day proceeded slower than planned. In the morning, the snow was firm, but as the day wore on it got mushy. On the summit around 3 PM, the students were tired. They had hoped to make it back to the Glen Alps Trailhead by 5 PM, but that would be impossible now. Some were concerned about rides, and others about congratulatory dinners waiting back in Anchorage. In the course, they had been taught that a hurried descent is never wise, but it appears that this fundamental hadn't taken hold with either the students or the two faculty members that day.

For me, June 29th was ideal for a sunny-evening jaunt into Chugach State Park, minutes from my house on Little Rabbit Creek. I drove to the Prospect Heights Trailhead, parked, shouldered a day pack with a few M&Ms and a water bottle and headed toward O'Malley Peak, a couple miles to the north of Ptarmigan Peak. My route happened to align with the path leading from the bottom of the Ptarmigan Peak couloir to the heliports of Anchorage's major hospitals.

My enjoyment of a perfectly sunny Alaska summer evening was soon punctuated by the sight and sound of helicopters overhead. They were from the Alaska National Guard rescue squadron, accompanied by another helicopter from the Alaska State Troopers. Because all of the choppers were traversing the route toward Powerline Pass, the shortest way from Anchorage to the Seward Highway and Portage, I surmised there had probably been a major motor vehicle accident on the other side of the peaks. The only thing that puzzled me was the number of helicopters. Even for a serious auto accident, usually only one helicopter is dispatched.

On Monday morning, June 30, an urgent investigative assignment arrived on my office desk. It came from UAA's risk manager. I dropped everything else and threw myself into this investigation. Loving the mountains and mountaineering, I was also gripped by angst to read what had happened to young women and men simply out cultivating their passion and seeking the "freedom of the hills."

I got permission from UAA Risk Management to charter a helicopter to fly to Ptarmigan Peak and photograph both where the climbers fell, and get an overall perspective of the rest of the north couloir. On the way to the heliport in Anchorage, I doglegged to my house to grab some mountaineering gear. Another adjuster joined me for the flight. I asked the pilot to first take us to Ptarmigan's summit. There he hovered over the area where the kids had relaxed and eaten a late lunch. The wind was calm, so he said he could put the helicopter down there, but I told him it would be more useful if he could do a few passes over the couloir to photograph and map-out the accident.

I would liken the flow of the couloir to a theme park roller coaster, narrow and dropping off fast from the top, then twisting first to the left and then to the right, coming perilously close to the rock cliffs. These were a jumble of metamorphic and volcanic tuffs, not at all like the more familiar smooth granite monoliths in places such as Yosemite. Instead, they formed a mammoth set of graters and meat-grinders. Below the top drop-off, about a third of the way down the 2,000-foot couloir, the slope gradually started to become less steep. If this couloir were a ski slope, it would be a double-black-diamond—experts only—on the top two-thirds. And even dare-devils would be wary of the cookie-cutter rocks at the side of the run.

Did the lateness of the day contribute to the decision not to place the time-robbing pickets and flukes in the snow on the upper sections of the couloir? The party opted instead for something that works best on gentler slopes. Here's how it went: only one or two on a rope team were to make facing-out plunge steps down, while the other teammates position themselves against the snow slope, which was just inches in front of their faces, digging their ice axes into the snow as far as they could so that they could hold on as tight as possible in case someone fell—which, sadly, several did again and again. The belayers were simply jerked backwards and out into the air by their falling classmates.

But the worst situation imaginable came when falling climbers higher up tangled their ropes with others who were laboring to descend below them. Ropes became thoroughly ensnarled, and the group soon became a mass of flailing ice-axes and screaming young women and men.

From the helicopter, I saw the gouges in the snow where the panicking students had tried to self-arrest, only to be pulled out of position when the rope went tight and jerked them aloft once again. Up near the summit ridge, I saw just a few troughs in the snow, but the lower down we flew, we came upon a segment where the slide markings led to a cliff face, resuming again below. Finally, the pilot landed in the meadow where the climbers' tents had been the day before.

I alighted from the helicopter, donned my boots, and grabbed my ice axe. I began kicking steps in the snow slope above the meadow to see what else I might discover on the lower mountain. I stopped when I glimpsed a silver reflection beside the toe of my right boot. It was a man's Bulova sports watch with a stainless-steel flex-band, showing the correct time. Who had worn this timepiece the day before? Had he been anxious before the fall? And what force of nature tore it from his wrist? I brought it back to be claimed by the owner. Or maybe not.

The next day at the office was July 1, and I started considering my birthday shindig. I had an Alaska Airlines flight that afternoon to Seattle, which was supposed to be followed by a drive to Lacey in a rental car. I had critical work to do in Anchorage. I couldn't possibly tell anyone that I had to go to my birthday party.

I changed my flight to the next night—a red-eye just before 1 AM on July 3. I didn't let anybody in Anchorage know what I was up to. Since I had been mostly away from the office during the course of the investigation, nobody would know where I was the day before a holiday. Bleary-eyed, I pulled into Mom and Dad's driveway. The big cake and the finger food were already spread out on the table. I had already told my parents what was up. The hideaway in the den was made up with sheets and a pillow. I conked out until Mom woke me to take a shower and prepare for the first arrivals at 2 PM.

The party was a success, but I felt awkwardly queasy in my conical party hat, considering the injuries and deaths that occupied my thoughts. After the last guest was out the door, I packed up my haul of birthday presents and drove north to Sea-Tac Airport and caught the evening flight back to Anchorage. The office was closed the next day for the Fourth, but I went in to work, anyway.

The initial investigation continued with interviews of various climbers either conducted in the hospital or elsewhere after they were released. Of all the stories, I was most affected by one young man, his face marred by multiple wounds closed with sutures. He told me how the rope went tight at his seat-harness and jerked him out of his hold on the ice axe. Since it was attached by a loop to his wrist, both he and the axe went flying backwards boots-over-head, and then head-over-boots. He felt as if he were in the air for a very long time—but he knew he wasn't. He was one of the 14 people in a heap of tangled ropes and bodies on the blood-stained snow slopes below the rock face. Bouncing and ricocheting off the rocks again and again was perhaps the greatest agony he'd ever experienced. When airborne between the impacts, he said he had just wished that his time in the air wouldn't cease. The place where the moaning climbers landed was a tangle of high-tech climbing gear, ropes, and bleeding bodies, some who were moving, and two who weren't. Those two young students had died of their injuries. Only one of the students had injuries superficial enough to be treated and released from the hospital that night. The rest were admitted either into hospital rooms or the ICU.

My contribution to this monumental investigation ended when nationally recognized authorities on mountain rescue stepped in. They came from Denali National Park, the Anchorage Fire Department, and from Lower 48 mountain rescue councils in Washington State and Colorado. The university retained legal consultants, too. Every step, every memo, every whisper, was scrutinized by plaintiffs' and defense attorneys. It was going to be several years before all the cases of the living and the dead would be closed.

Aside from the horrendous toll in young lives and blood seen on June 29, 1997, another sad casualty was that of the AWS 105 *Basic Mountaineering* course, which disappeared from future UAA catalogs. In my opinion, while there certainly were mistakes on Ptarmigan Peak, the students had received sound mountaineering instruction, and they were executing what they had been taught as well as they could. There were most certainly other mistakes that contributed to this tragedy, but the mountaineering investigators, not I, would be presenting those findings.

In the years since, my experience with multiple sclerosis (MS) has underlined the fact that my climbing days are over. Looking back, I consider myself lucky; the worst injury-accident I ever experienced wasn't bad. I had tumbled out of a self-arrest on steep snow, but fortunately there was good run-out at the bottom, so my body just slid to a stop. I discovered the reason for the pain when I felt inside my left pant leg and my index finger disappeared into a hole in my thigh. My ice axe had punched in between blood vessels, so the wound was fairly dry. A stop at an urgent-care clinic on the way back to the city was all the care I ended up needing. And because the accident happened on a high-up, pristine snow slope, there was little risk of bacterial infection.

The American Alpine Club (AAC) annually publishes its respected tome, *Accidents in North American Mountaineering,* for members. The summaries are brutal, but accurate.

In the AAC 1998 publication, once such summary appeared entitled *FALL ON SNOW, UNABLE TO SELF-ARREST, INADEQUATE PROTECTION, POOR POSITION, INEXPERIENCE, PTARMIGAN PEAK, CHUGACH STATE PARK.* The ponderous title is an adequate synopsis by itself, but the full article gives hundreds more details. What it doesn't touch upon though is the humanity of those who fell and the rescuers and first-responders who worked to save them.

I hope that the 12 survivors of the Ptarmigan Peak incident were ultimately able to return to the mountains. Some people label mountaineering—even as Queen Victoria did—a dangerous obsession that should be outlawed. Others see it as raw passion, an expression of humanity's soul. The photographer Ansel Adams famously said, *"In wilderness is the preservation of the world."* Any wild-lands mountaineer likely knows what Adams meant.

In Wilderness is the preservation of the world, Sharkfin Tower near Cascade Pass.

Appendices

Appendix One:
Slime Mold

At age 18, I was hiking in a climbers' party toward Glacier Peak, the volcano that gives the Glacier Peak Wilderness Area its name. Alongside the Suiattle River trail there were colonnades of eight-inch-high bunchberry dogwood running off in white floral serendipity into the Douglas fir undergrowth. The bunchberry dogwood soon became my favorite; however, it had competition from another mountain plant, similar in size, but festooned with hard, perfectly round, orange-red berries.

Decades later, I figured out that I only ever saw the white flowered bunchberry dogwood in the spring, while I saw that other red berried plant in August—*BINGO!* They were actually one in the same. This was a life lesson taught by a flower in the forest: Youth is beautiful but doesn't last. The maturity it spawns has the potential to be even better.

This Glacier Peak Wilderness Area in Washington State, under the jurisdiction of the U.S. Forest Service (USFS), was the outcome of a war between titans; Seattle-based conservationists vs. logging companies based in Tacoma, Washington, and Atlanta, Georgia. We preservationists wanted what we called "the American Alps" to become a national park that stretched from the Canadian border south to Stevens Pass.

The struggle was to stop the Forest Service from selling permits for clear-cutting the old-growth monarchs of the mountain wilderness. The USFS was operating under its deceptively benign-sounding doctrine of "multiple-use," nothing more than window-dressing for their plan to open timber sales all the way up to the rocks of the Cascades peaks. Logging behemoths such as Weyerhaeuser Timber manipulated the planning sessions of the lowly Forest Service government workers.

In those days, to satiate big timber companies, the USFS was preparing to sell billions of board feet stored in old-growth woodland giants either as whole logs to Asia or to U.S. mills that made plywood and dimensional building lumber. The operations that made such products were geared up to only accept big saw logs in those days. Small trees would be routed into the stinky chemical-soup of the pulp mills to come out as crisp, white paper. (Today's industry has tilted toward such things as oriented strand board [OSB] made from small trees, especially those that grow fast in the American South in places such as the mountains of Georgia, which have become the 21st century conservation battleground.)

But to their chagrin of the logging mega-giants, efforts of such groups as the North Cascades Conservation Council (NCCC) were winning public approval. The NCCC was born of leaders such as author Harvey Manning and the great photographers Bob and Ira Spring. Even as a 13-year-old entering junior high, I was captivated by the fight and entered in while pretending to be much older in my letters. After testifying on paper and in person, I would still have to wait until college for Congress to grant conservationists victory with its establishment of the 505,000-acre North Cascades National Park on October 2, 1968.

Even though the North Cascades National Park was less than half of what the NCCC had wanted, its very existence was a bitter defeat for the Forest Service for two reasons. It withdrew old-growth forest that they were planning to designate for industrial logging, and it meant that they had to cede territory to their arch enemy, the Department of the Interior. National Parks were part of the Interior Department, while everything else was run by the Forest Service as part of the Department of Agriculture.

But that wasn't the end of the story. The will of the people eventually prevailed in the campaign they had started to keep chainsaws away from the "gemstone of America's Wilderness Alps," Glacier Peak. In response, the Forest Service reluctantly conferred the newly created special status of *"Designated Wilderness"* on the Glacier Peak region of the Mt. Baker National Forest. While this meant that the Forest Service continued to hold title to the land, logging and motor vehicles were prohibited. Isaac Walton and John Muir would have been delighted with the victory for people who think not every tree should be felled and made into those crappy dining tables advertised on late-night TV.

As for the Glacier Peak climb I was taking part in as an 18-year-old, our climbing party comprised six people (two rope teams of three each for the summit push to come later). That day on the Suiattle River Trail, a congenial PhD in botany at the University of Washington was part of our little group. At the university he was in charge of a special class of plants, those used for the potential creation of helpful pharmaceuticals. He told me, for example, that the foxglove (digitalis), which I saw that day, was used to treat heart disease. He also explained how easy it is to recognize the cascara shrub during a summer of tent-caterpillar infestation. Those crawly little creepers stay away from that tree for the same reason that humans want its bark. It is a remedy for constipation, but one capable of giving caterpillars fatal diarrhea.

The star of that trail that day, however, were the slime molds. Easily overlooked, they appeared to be a kind of gooey fluff or maybe a dribble of mildewing pancake batter. I was surprised to learn from him that slime molds were widespread. This venerable botanist explained how they were taxonomically tough, as they didn't fit neatly into either the plant or animal kingdom. In other words, they could creep over and eat you if you were terribly slow or terribly dead, provided that you tasted a lot like their preferred food, oatmeal. Or if they were not in the animal-like-phase of their lives, they could appear to be nothing more than the contents of a supermarket bag of "*Fresh* Spring Salad Greens" five weeks past its pull date.

At the time I was hiking along the Suiattle River Trail, global research on slime molds had just begun at universities in Japan, France, and to a lesser extent, the United States. Botanists from around the world demonstrated that while slime molds are prominent examples of organisms that blur the line between plants and animals, they are not the only ones. As the Einsteins of the plant-animal grouping, they can reason, and this fact is a befuddling peculiarity given their lack of a brain.

I asked myself the same question about how one can function without a brain in regard to my sixth-grade teacher, Mr. Moran, at Mercer Crest Elementary School. He used to steal the extra cartons of milk from the lunchtime cart, thinking we milk-cart monitor boys didn't know how to count, or that 12-year-olds wouldn't be able to figure out we were two units short upon final tally.

Remember when the hippies of the sixties said you should sing to your petunias because they thrive on your goodwill? Well, they might not have been far off. In a 2022 article, Switzerland's *Neue Zürcher Zeitung* gave scientific evidence that trees under stress sense impending death. Some are seemingly lonely for others of their species. Also, when faced with polluted air and groundwater, they will fight valiantly for years, but eventually they just give up, kind of like when a 96-year-old decides they just don't want to go to their dialysis appointments anymore. Likewise, no amount of water and fertilizer will bring those trees back around once they've decided that being made into fireplace kindling wouldn't be such a bad fate after all.

As I have already explained, slime molds make logical projections and they can figure out the best route to dinner. This is not necessarily a straight line but the pathway with the greatest possibility of success. They might go all the way around the body of a dead botanist to dine on her last breakfast of oatmeal mush.

I would never call Republicans "slime molds" because I think those little guys—the molds, not the R's—are smarter than most in Congress. If you fear that you are reading machinations of a liberal, it's probably too late to get a refund of the price of this book. However, I equivocate by quoting Will Rogers, "I am not a member of any organized political party. I am a Democrat."

Another miscellaneous fact that I learned from botanists was how temperate rain forests function as a single organism. In other words, the moss depends on the other plants, and the fungal bodies upon the lichen, which itself is a symbiotic partnership of different organisms. In the temperate rain forests of coastal British Columbia, Washington, Oregon, and Southeast Alaska, there are at least 40 species of ferns, and they are just one of the intertwined groupings of botanical and biological interdependence.

In these rain forests you will also find pale jumping slugs (yes, there really is a slug that can jump, a fact that aroused Hitchcockian fear in me when camped at the Happy Four Shelter in the Hoh Rain Forest of

Olympic National Park). And don't forget the gaudily beautiful, stinky but edible skunk cabbage. If you want to bail on your girlfriend, give her a big bouquet of the stuff. It will likely be more effective than eating onions or failing to floss.

Just above the lowest understory of the forest is where the alders and vine maples flourish. Higher up, Sitka spruce and western red cedars can reach heights of up to 190 feet. This is just a start. Down on the ground near your hiking boots you will find the humble slime molds.

They all depend on one another. The fabled spotted owl lives high up in the coastal spruce trees, and only here because that bird is a part of the rain forest community. Anybody with an eye for grandeur, who is not distracted by a stock portfolio that includes plywood and paper companies, can find wonder in the rain forest. The Weyerhauser Timber Company has as its corporate motto: *avarus nothi semper vincere*, meaning "Greedy bastards always win." Their propagandists, whose offspring went on to tell the American public that cigarette smoking was healthful, bought full-page ads in magazines showing how clear-cutting of the rain forest mercifully gave those poor crammed-together trees room to grow.

But the science that remains cloistered with the company's researchers, never making it upstairs to the logging companies' board rooms, shows that clear-cutting can alter the weather system and send ocean storms in the opposite direction. If the rain forest managed to come back on its own as a viable ecosystem, it would take a thousand years. Reforestation is a good idea, but if you let the logging companies plant their seedlings, you end up with a single-species Christmas tree farm. No varied thrushes, banana slugs, eagles, or other members of the 8,500 species of creatures found in the temperate rain forests of the North.

Still, even before the last logging truck had left the clear cut, the slime molds would have figured out there was no future there and wandered off to a Forest Service guard station to see if they might be able to find some oatmeal spilled out of a kitchen cupboard.

Appendix Two:
M&Ms Are Life Savers

M&Ms were inspired by a confection intended to be included in soldiers' rations during the Spanish Civil War. Near its conclusion, on September 10, 1941, Forrest Mars and Bruce Murrie created a chocolate shaped like mini lenses encased in candy shells to make them easy to transport without concern about the temperatures in cargo holds. That original selling-point continued with the proposition that this was—as the jingle went—*"Milk chocolate that melts in your mouth, not in your hand."*

However, during a fourth-grade spelling test when I secreted some M&Ms in my right hand while writing with my left (I'm a lefty), my sweaty palm was stained red, green, yellow, and brown. Millions of students around the world assert that M&Ms are a perfect desktop brain food. But they didn't help me on that spelling quiz. Mrs. Geibel dictated *THEE-ATE-UR*. But the previous Saturday, Mom had driven a bunch of us kids from Mercer Island to see *Francis the Talking Mule* at the Issaquah Theatre. So, I spelled it the way it was written on the neon marquis, *"Theatre."*

We exchanged papers for grading, and Samantha marked me wrong. Not possible! I never get anything but perfect marks in spelling! I marched to Mrs. Geibel's desk. With brutal lack of compassion, she intoned, "Go back to you seat, Kris. Nine out of ten isn't bad." The only other time I was so mortified was when I did make a bona fide error. We had a unit on the names of residents of localities around the world: New York, *New Yorker*. Texas, *Texan*. Moscow, *Muscovite*. The teacher erupted into humiliating laughter when she graded my paper. For Paris, I had written what some detractors would say was correct, *Parisite*.

The original M&Ms supposedly included the color purple. I never saw one of those, so I think that's apocryphal information. In the Old Testament, the food that mysteriously appeared every morning to feed the Israelites in the wilderness was called "manna."

That six-day-a-week miracle provided perfect sustenance, perhaps even better than Continental Baking Company's *Wonder Bread*, whose ads insisted, *"Builds strong bodies twelve ways."*

Some American fundamentalist Christians have named their churches after this Bible *Wonder-Food*, with names such as "Bread of Heaven Chapel," I don't know how good the manna was in Bible times, but I suspect it didn't taste like M&Ms, because the Bible tells us that the Israelites got sick of it. Who could ever tire of M&Ms?

The following story of a miracle isn't biblical, and it doesn't involve candy-coated milk-chocolate, but something very close. I made my first climb of Mount Adams (a 12,281-foot strato-volcano in southcentral Washington State) when I was 15. I hadn't yet learned the importance of constantly snacking while burning calories ascending mountain snow hour after hour in the cold and at high altitude. A raw wind was blowing so hard that it was tough to hear what the others said. Exertion in the diminished oxygen and decreased air pressure of the heights brings on feebleness, nausea, and tremors. At extreme high altitudes such as on Denali or Everest, this mountain sickness becomes the often-fatal cough and drowning-sensation of HAPE, "high altitude pulmonary edema."

On Adams, I was the youngest in our climbing party. We kicked cramponed steps in the ice up to the false summit, where we threw down our packs for a rest break. One of our party was a physician, who had seen me stumble. He reached into his first aid kit and produced a package of foil-wrapped wafers of glucose. He motioned for me to come over to him, but I was so weak at that moment I had to crawl on my hands and knees across the volcanic scoria and ice to reach him. He handed me several squares of this actual melt-in-your-mouth sugar. With one follow-up swig from my water bottle, a miracle took place. A pulse of heat coursed through my body's core and first hit my head and face, then my hands, and finally my legs and feet. The latter had grown numb because the metal crampons had been transmitting the cold of the ice to my boots. My toes were the last to warm up, but the glucose high had enabled me to push onward to the summit.

Afterwards, I couldn't find medical-grade glucose in the supermarket, but I already knew its close relative. When one's body is craving glucose-sugar, M&Ms can generate a similar ether-into-the-carburetor kick after a conversion in the stomach—faster than anything that ever happens during a church's altar call—converts the sucrose into glucose and fructose.

Years later, I was older but not wiser by virtue of parenthood—and that detail is important to this story because I knew nothing yet about the metabolism of little boys. Hiking buddy Bill Eldridge wanted to take his two sons David, age 12, and Matt, age 7, on an overnight hike on a section of Mount Rainier's Wonderland Trail, a segment of the legendary circumnavigation of this great Pacific Northwest volcano and all its 26 glaciers.

Bill was slated to carry an enormous pack with tent, food, and other gear, while his sons got away with nearly empty packs that were too big for their young bodies. I, on the other hand, had in my *Schönhofen* internal-frame pack a snazzy MSR stove, and my *Omnipotent*, a mountaineering tent that was the best and lightest of its kind at the time.

On the first day, we started from the Box Canyon trailhead and began to work our way toward Indian Bar. For kids of any age, one of the highlights of backpacking is taking breaks. An hour into the hike, we plopped down on some boulders near the trail and slipped out of our packs. I knew that a backpacker or a climber should have snacks in nearly every pocket. This time, however, because I wouldn't be burning so many calories, I decided on just one snacking decadence in addition to meals for this two-day trip. I bought the biggest bag of M&Ms that Albertsons had. If I paced myself, I would probably still have a handful left by the time we descended to the Frying Pan Creek trailhead.

So, on that second hour of the first day of our trip, I tore the corner off the M&Ms bag. Two sets of young eyes laser-burned onto the M&Ms. David and Mathew intoned in unison, "Mr. Erickson, can we have some?" "Sure," I said, and handed them the bag and turned to discuss the trail ahead with Bill. If I had known better, I would have said, "Sure. Put your hands out," and then poured a little pile into each boy's hands.

It was time to shoulder our packs again. I looked for the M&Ms to put the bag back inside my pack. It wasn't there because David and Matt were still feeding. Those munching machines had made the previously bulging bag look like it was miniature version of Jared after he lost 245 pounds by eating at Subway. I was too surprised at what the little mouths had accomplished in those 10 minutes to wonder if they might take off under the influence of a sugar overdose or just puke.

The hike went well after that. It was great fun in perfect weather, and I didn't have to worry about the temptation to snack on too many more M&Ms.

Postscript

I asked Matt, who gave me this photo, to review the M&Ms story for accuracy. Today, he and his wife live near Black Diamond, Washington. Sadly, both David and the boys' father Bill, have departed this earth for a realm far beyond the mountains. But maybe when Matt and I join them someday, we will all share some manna M&Ms.

David and Matt Eldridge at Cape Alava in the Olympic National Park's Ocean Strip, photo by their father, Bill Eldridge.

Thank-Yous

In the last five decades, hundreds of people have said I have to write a book about the adventures I have fallen into. *Blood Piss & Cheer ALASKA* is a compendium of just some of those stories. My thanks go to each one of you who has encouraged me to write. Here are a few shout-outs to people that have worked directly on this latest book:

Evan Erickson, my son, is a broadcast journalist, writer, and freelancer who has plied his trade from Beijing, China to Yangon, Myanmar to Tbilisi, Georgia; and now he is in another exotic place, Bethel, Alaska. Evan's wanderlust and spirit of adventure have taken him from charity work in Thailand to commercial fishing in Alaskan waters to climbing in China to trekking in the Himalayan forelands of India. Evan has edited thousands upon thousands of pages of academic pages written by Chinese graduate students seeking to have their works appear in good English, and my writing, too, has profited from his exactitude, for which I am exceedingly grateful.

Marc Heriot came to work with me in Community Chapel Publications as a photographer and graphics artist when he was barely 20. During his careers in management of graphic artists and print media for Bellevue College and then as an analytical project manager at KPMG, Marc has proved his versatility. On top of that, he is exceedingly kind. You see his name as the designer of the cover, but in addition to that, both he and his wife, Diane, provided insights and textual edits that moved the book toward completion.

Lizzie Newell is an Anchorage friend who is an author herself knows writing backwards, forwards, and sideways. She is in a writers' guild and is regularly in touch with other crafters of books across North America. As Marc Heriot pointed out to me, "Kristian, you are fortunate to have Lizzie on the team producing this book." Indeed I am!

Barbara Richards. I first glimpsed Barb across the dining room at a PLU student government conference in October 1965. When I heard her speak, I was instantly intrigued with this talented woman. We have known each other ever since. Barb graduated in nursing, and in her storied career she taught others compassionate care of single moms and their children. Barb knows good, she knows practical, and she knows kind. And this book has benefited from her comments.

Matt Eldridge loves the mountains as much as I do, and that is saying a lot. And in alpine meadows he knows how to differentiate between the diminutive alpine avalanche lilies and avalanche fawn lilies (both white), and the glacier lilies (yellow). Matt is the younger brother in the M&Ms story that you just read. It is my privilege to know Matt as both an inspiration and a textual contributor to this book.

My Alaskan dream seen under an October moon.

Made in the USA
Columbia, SC
13 May 2024

7992652a-bf2b-448d-b9f3-5883f2e82e24R01